Taking Back My Soul:
Health and Healing

Edited and Co-Authored by

Demetria Hill Cannady, PhD, LPC
A Work In Progress, LLC
Valdosta, Georgia

Taking My Soul Back: Health and Healing

Published by:

A Work In Progress, LLC
Valdosta, Georgia 31601
(478) 227-7299
www.dhcann.09@gmail.com

ISBN: 978-0-692-10416-3

Cover Photo Credit: Jamon Williams Photography
Editing: Nicole Cooper

Printed in the United States of America

Table of Contents

Foreword
Demetria Hill Cannady, PhD, LPC, MAC

As women, we often sacrifice ourselves for the greater good of others. Women will walk around with years of resentment, disappointment, hurt, and pain as not to hurt others, primarily family members that have physically and/or mentally hurt us and as to not cast a light on ourselves and what we experienced. Through numerous years of providing counseling services to women, many have elected to keep the most painful memories and hurts to themselves. They sometimes disclose these painful memories in a counseling session after holding themselves in bondage for a lifetime. When asked why they never told anyone, the responses are normally surrounded by fear: fear of being judged, fear of being labeled, fear of backlash, fear of rejection, fear of the unknown, and fear in general. Fear keeps us all in bondage.

Our ancestors taught us, "What happens in this house stays in this house," therefore many never told anyone about the trauma they endured, especially if the trauma occurred from a family member or the friends of a family member. However, their actions following the trauma spoke volumes, whether through "acting out," anger, promiscuity, or becoming withdrawn. Not knowing the root of the problem many women have been labeled as "loose," "fast," "mean," etc. I recently asked a question of women, "Does time heal all wounds?" There were a variety of answers; yes, no, and sometimes. Some answers, "Yes but there's more to healing than time;" "Sometimes because things such as death or lack of relationships leaves a lasting effect;" "No but time makes it easier to manage but not heal;" "Yes if the wound is fixable but the tongue can be damaging; think twice react once;"

Additional responses: "Yes with time, honest communication (about feelings), forgiveness, therapy or a neutral person who has professional knowledge about that which has hurt you;" "Time along with therapeutic interventions;" "No you just learn to deal with the pain;" No you just learn to cope;" "I just don't believe that time heals all wounds;" "Healing comes from God but only when we're ready and willing to accept what's happened and get to work going through the process of becoming better;" "God dispenses time. It's like a wound care center and the wounds are healing from the inside out;" "Nope time provides a scab which gets rubbed off every now and then. Your reaction determines whether it festers or mends. Therapy can be the ointment."

Through the answers presented it appears that we have not given ourselves permission to grieve what was taken away from us nor let go of these hurts and heal but we have given ourselves permission to keep silent and to continue to live with these awful memories and decades of hurts, most which have occurred by no faults of our own. We must give ourselves permission to heal. Release these decades of hurt and begin to live your best life. Become the person you were intended to be, your authentic self!

Introduction

Demetria Hill Cannady, PhD, LPC

While formulating this book which is much different than the first book, *Authentic Tales of Seven Women: The Truth of Who I Am,* this book has a theme throughout by no doing from myself or the co-authors in this book. The themes of this book were along the lines of depression and grief and the fact that their spiritual beliefs and upbringing held all the pieces together in the worst of times. African Americans, especially women have always looked to spirituality during challenging times. We have been known to use prayer and increase spirituality to cope with stress, trauma, and mental illness. Spirituality, as defined by Merriam-Webster Dictionary, is something that in ecclesiastical law belongs to the church or to a cleric; clergy; sensitivity or attachment to religious values; the quality or state of being spiritual. The University of Maryland Medical Center stated, "Spirituality has been defined in numerous ways, including a belief in a power operating in the universe that is greater than oneself, a sense of interconnectedness with all living creatures, and an awareness of the purpose and meaning of life and the development of personal values. It is the way you find meaning hope, comfort, and inner peace in your life.

Spirituality often assists us with finding meaning and the purpose for our lives, the "bigger picture." Oprah Winfrey defined spirituality as "the essence of who you are." Although spirituality is often associated with religion, personal spirituality can be developed through music, art, or a connection with nature. People also find spirituality through acts of compassion and selflessness. Spirituality presents us with hope when things appear bleak and encourages us to be our best and most authentic self by supplying us with biblical principles to live by, focusing on the Ten Commandments. Spirituality is medication for the heart and spirit and therapy is deemed medicine for the mind and in some instances the soul.

Social Justice and Mental Health

In completing my research for this book, I was reminded through journal articles that mental illness is a social justice issue. Mental illness has such a stigma attached to it that it's a social issue that is rarely discussed unless the discussion consists of budget cuts and/or someone being shot or killed because law enforcement wasn't aware that there were mental health issues present. As I continued the research I was able to locate a number of social injustices as it related to mental illness: failed mental health system; mentally ill people being shot/killed; being institutionalized/ incarcerated; stereotypes of people with significant mental illnesses; little to no support of individuals who have mental illnesses; rural areas with little to no resources for individuals with mental illness; the ER is used in times of crisis for individuals with mental illness, individuals being over or under medicated; limited education for individuals/ community on mental illness; continuum of care; and the benefits of early intervention (www.publichealthreviews.bloomedcentral.com/articles).

Reflecting to slavery, African Americans have been traumatized since the beginning. Our ancestors received mental, emotional, physical, and sexual abuse; probably not termed this during the slavery era, I'm sure. From then to now, we, as a people, continue to experience trauma and/or be haunted from things which have occurred in our past. Within one of the chapters, one of the ladies mentions about the slaves not being able to shed tears and if tears were shed, they would be beaten until the tears were no more.

Poverty and Mental Health

One may question, why the topic of poverty and mental health? Poverty and mental health correlate with each other because individuals with mental health issues have challenges such as difficulty with finances, homelessness, hunger, obtaining/taking medications consistently, stability in the workforce, or just getting their basic needs met, in general. "There are nearly 34 million people who identify themselves as African Americans, 22% of them live in poverty. These individuals are at risk for mental illness due to a sizeable number of them being homeless, incarcerated, being involved with Department of Family and Children Services, and/or victims of serious and violent crimes," [Surgeon General's Report: Mental Health, Cultural, Race, Ethnicity, 2001].

Forty percent of youth are in the criminal justice system, and forty-five percent are in foster care. Children in foster care exhibit behaviors of aggression, fighting, negativism, and isolation [APA, Monitor of Psychology, 2005]. Over twenty-five percent of African Americans have been exposed to violence and are at risk for having Post Traumatic Stress Disorder. African Americans are twice as likely to be diagnosed with Schizophrenia [Mental Health Services Research, 2000]. In 2005 Census, African Americans were 7.3 times more likely to live in extreme poverty neighborhoods with limited access to mental health services. American Psychiatric Association reports that as many as 1 in 4 adults in the United States will suffer from a mental health issue. Twenty percent more African Americans are more likely to report having psychological distress than non-Hispanic Whites which has been reported by the Department of Health and Human Services. Those below the poverty line are three times more likely to experience psychological distress than those who are comfortably above the poverty lines (www.mic.com/articles). These figures were from several years ago, so the numbers and percentages are higher, which confirms more research needs to be completed, more frequently.

REFERENCES:

American Psychological Association, 2005. African Americans have limited access to mental and behavioral health care. *Monitor of Psychology*. Retrieved from: http://www.apa.org/about/gr/issues/minority/access.aspx

Mental Health Services Research, 2000. Access and Cost Barriers to Mental Health Care by Insurance Status, 1999 to 2010. Retrieved from: https://www.ncbi.nlm.nih.gov/pmc/articles/PMC4236908/

Poverty and Mental Health. Retrieved from: www.mic.com/articles.

Social Justice and Mental Health. www.publichealthreviews.bloomedcentral.com/articles

Surgeon General's Report: Mental Health, Cultural, Race, Ethnicity, 2001. Retrieved from: https://profiles.nlm.nih.gov/ps/retrieve/ResourceMetadata/NNBBHS.

The Inspirational Treasure, Shalonda Williams-McClendon, is one who has truly lived her ministry beforehand. She uses her gifts, skills and spiritual calling to impact women across the globe to find the true treasure; the true value within. This prophetess, minister, inspirational speaker, certified life coach and author has spent the past 20+ year finding that God given value within herself. Her own story of hopelessness, homelessness, promiscuity and deliverance has already helped thousands to be liberated. Shalonda has decided to use her experiences and godly insight to help inspire women everywhere until wholeness is achieved.

www.lovewalkoutreach.org
www.facebook.com/coachtreasure
www.facebook.com/lovewalkoutreach
www.twitter.com/coach_treasure
www.instagram.com/coachtreasure
Periscope @NspirationalTreasure

Give Me My S.O.U.L. Back

Prophetess Shalonda "Treasure" Williams McClendon

Back In The Day

"Back in the day when I was young, I'm not a kid anymore, but some days I sit and wish I was a kid again", are some of the lyrics from the song titled "Back In The Day," by rapper Ahmad. When this song came out in 1994 I was still a kid, so it did not mean much to me. It was not until later in life, when I heard it that I would nod my head and begin to feel it. The truth is that I do not really remember any of his rap to the song. I only know the hook. Each time I hear it I vibe to the music and allow my thoughts to go "back in the day." As I sit here, considering where to start with this chapter, I begin to ask myself, "Do you really want to start back then?" This may seem a strange question, but it is a logical one to me because in hindsight, my "back in the day" was a mixture of woes, confusion, instability, bullying, church, trying to fit in, yelling and arguing and love. I am not sure where all the pieces should fit or what had the biggest effect on my mental situation.

"Back in the day," I was the girl that wanted to love everybody and wanted to fit in, but also the one that was always the new girl, so nobody wanted to accept me. I was the new girl at school, at church, married into a family, and even at the babysitters. It is easy to imagine watching a little girl like this on a movie. Everyone has sympathy for her and want to grab her up and show her lots of care. She is the one who runs home after being bullied at school and just falls on her bed crying her eyes out until someone comes to see about her… If there is someone there at all. I was, indeed, that girl.

Is this where the depression started though? I am not completely sure. When I try to think of a time in childhood when I was truly happy and excited to be a kid like normal people, I cannot think of a time. I remember smiling from time to time. I can conjure up thoughts of being loved by my mom and siblings as well. Mostly, however, what I see when I close my eyes are times when I was shunned, talked about and treated like I was the plague by others my age. As a kid, it does not matter if your family loves you if nobody else even cares that you are alive.

If I thought a bit harder, I'm sure that I can come up with a few occasions where I was genuinely joyful. The negative things scream so loud sometimes that the good stuff gets jammed way back in the background. "Back in the day" when I was young, I'm not a kid anymore but some days I sit in wish that I could have a redo so that I can be a kid. I believe childhood was where it started; Being bullied, molested, moved from house to house – thus school to school -, and constantly being rejected will do that to a soul.

The times when I was remotely happy was when I was singing in a choir or at my grandfather's holiness church. They would be in church all day and that was just fine for me because I loved the fast-paced music and watching my aunts and cousins shout. That scene made me feel alive and there I was accepted. It was strange. That was my biological fathers side of the family so because I did not see them often it felt like I was being welcomed and loved on by strangers. This was the type of love I wanted from the other strangers I encountered. Needless to say, this was not all the time so this "high" did not last for long. The only other time that I felt a little happiness was when… hold on, I will wait to tell that part. For now, I am pretty sure, just from writing my own words, that "back in the day" is when my mental "situation" started. It is, honestly, so blotchy when I think back, that I am more than sure that is the beginning of my story.

Intimacy Misunderstood

Someone once said that intimacy spoken slowly would be "In-To-Me-I-See". It's a cute play on the word, but it wasn't my truth back then. I did not see into myself at all. All I saw was what others thought of me.

The word intimacy, according to Google, means close familiarity or closeness. I suppose that this is what I was looking for from the others around me. I wanted them to see into me. I wanted people to see that I was likable and that I had a good heart and just wanted to be their friend. As a child, I did not really understand a child's way of thinking. More often than not, kids only wanted to play with people they were familiar with, so when a new face came, everybody became super territorial. That may just be the reason that I became a chaser.

I was not the type to physically chase a person down and make them be my friend. I guess that it may have felt that way to them because I became a bit pushy and a lot needy when it came to attention. I had a few people that "liked" me as a person, but it was the ones who pushed me off that I wanted to see me. Maybe it was some sort of challenge for me. It could be that because I felt so rejected, I would do anything to be desired by those who did not want me.

Thinking about this makes me think of the other times when I felt a bit of happiness. It was when boys were paying me attention. That attention did not have to be positive like two buddies playing together. It could have been when they grabbed my behind or when they tried to touch me in private places. It was all good as far as I was concerned. Attention was attention to me. This had to be intimacy, right? They were close to me, in a way. At least they liked something about me.

What is very interesting is that this type of attention started for me long before I was old enough to understand any of it. A visit with some family members turned into the beginning an inner war that I was in NO way prepared to handle. A dream of me running up a dark lane turned into me waking up just as my cousin was putting my covers back on me. I was only six years old, so I had no idea what was happening. All I knew is that I felt a little funny down there.

After that first dream, I would have that exact same dream every night until I went back home to my mommy. It wasn't until the day when we were on our way to Walt Disney World that I really knew that something was happening. Again, I did not understand it. I was scared, to be honest. I didn't really know that it was something wrong but the "shhhhh" finger going up to his mouth was a good indicator that I was not supposed to tell. On the way to Walt Disney World, we had to make a stop for my aunts to go to a meeting. We were told to stay in the car and not to move. We knew what that meant. We had our snacks and things to keep us busy. I do not remember what snacks I got from the store. I do, however, remember what he had. I remember the Crunch and Munch because I wanted some, and he would not let me have any until I did him a "favor".

Yes, indeed, there was reason to be a depressed little girl, chasing people around just to say that you conquered rejection.

It became common though. I believe this is also where the spirit of jealousy came from. He showed me all the attention in the house, but when we got around other kids, especially girls, he would act funny with me. He no longer favored me or even touched me. As a matter of fact, he was often very mean to me. Could this be why I always desired to get the attention of the ones who paid me no attention? Could this be the reason why, if there wasn't any touching or any church music, I was straight up unhappy?

Participation Limited

At one point, I would go to my aunt and uncle every other summer. Eventually the visits stopped all together. By the time they stopped the visits, I was all the way turned out. I do not remember him ever having sex with me. As far as I know, it was only a touch. Obviously, some seriously firm touching for it to feel that funny down there, but only God knows. I was in a dream state, so I honestly don't know. I do know that I was totally infatuated with my adopted cousin, and he was infatuated with me as long as no one else was around. After the "favor" he asked of me, he became bolder about the touching. He would do it even while I was awake. At first, I did not tell because I was scared, but later I kept it a secret because I didn't want anyone to try to stop it.

I had no idea that this time in my life would be the foundation of my making. That is definitely what it appeared to be for most of my life. My participation in anything that was not church, music or boys was very limited. Boys were the most thought-consuming of them all though. Even when I was at church and singing, if someone wasn't flirting with me, I was miserable. Passing love letters and sneaking to the bathroom for a hug was only a part of it. It was way too much, but it was my normal. I shake my head at the thought now. This feeling that was brought forth in me had me writing love poems and singing the blue at twelve years old.

To say the least, where my mind was, was totally crazy at that age. The worse part of it is that I remember how I felt when a boy I liked chose another girl. It wasn't the typical girly-girl irritation. It was rage and disgust. I felt, every time, like my life was completely over.

Was it because of the molestation alone that I found my way to this mental "situation" called depression? It could have been. Come to think of it, most of what I experienced after six years old, even the shunning, may have been the result of this. I was the girl who wouldn't dance at parties because I felt too shy. I was afraid that people would laugh at my dancing or that it would give people another reason not to like me. I was the girl who would do what people told me to do just so I could try to be their "friend." I used to bring the 3rd grade bully candy, so he would like me. I even became a bully for about two seconds because I thought that it would make the 5th grade tough girls want to hang with me. That didn't last long though.

In hindsight, I had a lot of gifts and talents. I could sing, write poetry, run track, and I was very smart. I could have been doing anything else with my time. My mother was a librarian, so it was her life's mission to make me go to church and read. I hated the latter. I could have done something more than just sit at home and think about who didn't like me and how I could make them like me. My participation in life was so limited that even the things I would normally have enjoyed doing ceased to get my attention. By the time I was 13 years old, not only was I sad most of the time, my legs and muscles were always hurting, and I never felt good. Inside the house is where I was most of the time.

Obviously, It's Not Obvious

You would think that my mom would have noticed some things when I was younger, but she didn't. I guess she really had no reason to suspect anything. I was always a little different and definitely an "old soul." My mom was 30 years old, and my biological father was 41 years old when I was born. My oldest sibling was already twenty years old or very close to it by then. My mother's oldest child was fourteen years old. Next to me my mom had a son that was already eleven years old, and my dad had a daughter that was eight years old. I was born to stand out, I reckon. Therefore, if I acted a little older than I was, she had no real reason to think that it was because I had been being molested since I was six years old. On the other hand, if she did know, it would have messed up everything. She would have said something, and my attention would have stopped.

That sounds so pitiful, I know, but it was my truth "back in the day." Another part of my truth is that I would also gain a low tolerance for the same ones I was trying to get attention from. I was so messed up and confused as a kid. On the one hand, I wanted to be liked and accepted, and on the other hand, I was getting tired of fighting for the attention. I was also dealing with moving from place to place and always having to say goodbye when I finally felt secure. There was also the fact that the arguing and yelling that was going on at home was way too much. They carried him in super drunk from the lodge meeting, and he would wake up cursing and ranting at mommy. I would lie in the bed thinking the most horrible thoughts in those times.

As I got older, I grew a bit more bitter. I believe that I became an introvert of sorts, but it was not for the good. I don't know if some really understand how dangerous it is to be alone with your own thoughts when all of them are either negative or not healthy. I am more than sure now that the depression started even before I understood what it all meant.

To a child psychologist, my symptoms may have seemed obvious. They would have talked to me for a few minutes and established that I was too young to be that sad and introverted suddenly. Obviously, it was not obvious to those around me. I, honestly, believe that my mom was hurt and tired of going through so much with relationships. When we were living by ourselves, it was different. She was more at peace. When she was in a relationship, she did all she could to make things work and last. She stayed in marriages that were not so great for her for years at a time. Most days she took the low road or the godly wife role and just listened as the rants went on. Some days she just had to say something back. She was fed up, and I was screaming inside.

What was obvious to me was that I was not going to take all that from no boy. What wasn't obvious to me, at the time, was that this mindset would lead to many, many partners. I wanted the attention and intimacy so badly, but at the same time, I had a low tolerance for disrespect and drama. I stayed in relationships if things were okay. Five months of issues in a relationship was long-suffering enough for me. My numbers climbed up so high that I was embarrassed. The molestation, the need for attention, the rejection, the emotional abuse that I witnessed, the bullying, and now, the promiscuous behaviors had my world turned wayward. Was this reason enough for the depression to take over and remain with me? Obviously.

Let Me Explain

Comedian, Kevin Hart, has a comedy special where he uses the medicine of laughter to explain about some of his life's bad decisions. In this stand up, he speaks about his failed marriage and what he did to contribute to that. He speaks of other things that will keep a person laughing from the time it starts until the time it ends. I often wonder; however, would he be able to discuss it all in a regular setting where laughs were not the goal? How about—has he ever done so? If he has, I'm sure that it wasn't the easiest thing to do. It is never easy when you must cut through the first layers of your very negative past.

As a minister, I often share my testimony with those that listen on as I preach or teach. The Bible tells us that we overcome by the blood of the lamb, which is Jesus Christ, and by the word of our testimony. I believe that others are helped to overcome their circumstances, as well, when they hear the words and can relate. When I receive inboxes and emails telling me how something that I have said changed the way they see life, I rejoice. What I have come to know, however, is that, it is more about the sharing of my triumphs than it is about the woes. What I mean is this: anyone can tell you their "woe-is-me" story. It is great when there are those who can understand because they have been through similar things. Yet, it is something inspiring about a person who has been in it and through it who have made it out in joy.

It is not just about what I have gone through that have people eager to listen or even be coached by me. It is the explanation of the process that I endured to say that I am now free. Let me explain what I mean by giving a couple of scenarios. A pastor gets up every Sunday and begins to read the scripture behind his sermon. He read the verses, and then he tells the topic of his message. He starts off by sharing background from the text he's read, but before long he goes on to tell about his own experiences. Every experience that he shares is engaging, and it even makes the congregation laugh. He rounds the message up by simply saying, "But I'm not that way anymore since Jesus came into my life. Everyone stand, the doors of the church are open."

On the other side of town, there is a pastor who stands up to give his message for the day. He says a quick prayer, reads the passage of scripture that inspired his message, then gives the title. He begins with a story that goes like this: "There was a young man that grew up in my neighborhood when I was just a boy myself. He was always in trouble with the law. He was heavy into doing some of everything, from stealing cars to pimping prostitutes. He had no shame, and the entire neighbor feared him for some reason. It wasn't long until this young man took notice of me and begin to come after me to learn his lifestyle. He said that he liked me and thought I would make a great business man someday. The way that everyone was so scared of him I thought he would be mad when I turned him down, but he wasn't. He simply nodded his head and told me that he understood."

"One day when I got home from school, I heard a noise on the inside of door. It sounded like my mother was screaming, so I rushed in to see what was wrong. When I opened the door, the young man was standing over my mother choking her. He looked up at me and said, 'Do you want to rethink my offer'? At that moment, I did not fill up with fear, I filled up on anger. Looking at my mom's face turn blue, I knew that I had to say yes. From that day forward, I began to work for him. I stole cars from old ladies, I made runs for him delivering drugs, I would go get the men that would be the tricks for his girls, and I would beat up drug addicts that owed him money. I had turned wicked overnight. My anger kept me driven. I became cold, and I didn't care about anything or anybody accept my mama. If I kept going with this, he would keep my mother alive."

"I was depressed every day and even suicidal. Life made no sense. I knew things had gotten bad when I ended up beating one of the drug addicts so bad that he was put in a coma. I wanted to die. Then one day my grandmother came to visit. She saw me running the streets and told me that I was going to church with her and mama that next Sunday. I hated it. I didn't understand anything about it. Oddly enough, my only thought while I was sitting in church was about how much money I was missing out on. When I left church that day, I ran to the spot and didn't come home for two days. When I walked in, my mom was crying and ran to me to hug me. My grandmother was so angry that she started hitting me over and over again. 'You will not be like your daddy. You are better than that. He got you out there trying to make you just like him, but, you will not be that. I will take you away from here myself first,' Grand mama said. I was stuck on the 'your daddy... he got you out there' part."

"Come to find out, that young man was my dad. My mama never told me because she didn't want me to follow in his footsteps. The next Sunday, my grandmother made me go back to church. For some reason, this time, I listened. The man that stood up and started talking about family curses and how the sins of the father can be passed to the son. I felt tears come down my face. Before I knew it, I was walking up to the front for prayer or something. After that day, I decided that I would not be that person anymore. It had been ten years since that day he tried to kill my mom."

"I had done so much that I didn't even know how to start over. I was no longer a boy, I was a young man now myself. But, I was determined. I told my mom that I wanted us to go with grand mama and start over. From there I went back to school to get my diploma, I went into the military, and I continued to walk with God. It wasn't easy. I wanted to go back to the fast money. I wanted to stay angry and get my revenge on my dad. But, I kept praying and kept working hard to get out of the place I was in. I will never regret that decision."

After the pastor finishes with his story, he tells the congregation that it is because of God loving him so much that he could get it right, and then he opens the doors of the church. That day five young men and a young lady come and give their lives to the Lord.

I know that this was a long scenario, but, do you see the difference between sharing the woes and the drama and the explanation of how you got from where you were to where you are now? The explanation helps to save a life or two.

Abnormal Was My Normal

The preachers in the above scenarios were made up. but I have an explanation to share. I do not have any excuses as to what depression, molestation, bullying, rejection or instability made me do. I will say that when I look back on all that transpired, and I try to put into words what my soul (mind) was like back then, it sounds just as jumbled as I felt. My abnormal life was my normal. Being touched by my molester, and later, other boys and men, became commonplace and acceptable to me. I was so used to being rejected and not liked that once realized what my "power" was, and I used it, more often than not, to keep people around. Most of my life was a big hazy mess made up of woes.

Later, I understood that my mother stayed in situations, so that I wouldn't continue to be unstable. Yet, she couldn't stay in them because they weren't healthy for us. For a long time, I did not get it. I hated being the new girl and being bullied for being the new girl. I didn't like moving, but I didn't want to stay in the environment with the fussing and cursing. I couldn't go to visit any of my mother's friends who had daughters because most of them had brothers who were made to touch me or dry hump me. It was a lot. Most of which my mother did not know about. She tried so hard to keep me safe, but, sadly, was unaware that I was tainted and a sad little girl.

Shalonda, You Are Chosen

Remember me saying that I loved going to my grandfather's holiness church? I really loved it. It was one of the places that I felt great. Well, I believe that the love for it was infused in me from birth. It was the thing that would keep calling to me. God was there, and He wanted me to see His love for me, and He wanted me to love Him back. I knew that it was a great feeling, but I didn't know what else it was. God was calling to me from the feeling I would get inside. He had other people tell me that I was going to be a preacher and a prophet. I knew it sounded great, but it could not have been true with all that I had done. The thought of that made me even more sad. Of course, I thought it was sadness when it was really something so much deeper. Nevertheless, God kept sending people to tell me that I was chosen.

One would think that the feeling and the messages of being chosen would be enough to stop me from doing what I had begun doing. By the age of 13 years old, I was no longer a virgin, and I was so out there after. I was having so much sex that it was a wonder that I didn't get pregnant before the time that I did. I was careless, and most times, I didn't even use protection. At fifteen years old, I had a boyfriend that was twenty years old, and he turned me "all the way out." He was teaching me things that I should not have known. It was around that time that I realized that if I wasn't with a man, I was very miserable. More depression indeed. By this time, I was smoking weed and drinking. All my friends were older, so they could buy the alcohol. At the end of my sophomore year in high school, my sister came to visit and asked me if I wanted to come live with her in New York. This, I felt, was something I needed to do.

I lived in New York for my last two years of high school. I left there and moved to Tuskegee, AL for college and acted out some more. I ended up with a 1.9 G.P.A. the first semester. It's funny now, but it was nowhere near funny back then. Second semester, I did manage a 3.9 G.P.A. but my average was still not enough to allow me to keep my financial aid. Woe was me.

When I returned home that summer, I didn't know right away that I would not be returning to school. I left all my things in Alabama with my friend in hopes that we would be getting an apartment together. I came home and started going back to my childhood church, and there I met a man that would be my first real undoing. Previously, I dated a man that was five years older, but this was on a different level. I was eighteen; he was 33. He was the musician at the church now, and he owned a Convertible. He was always dressed in the best. I was more than infatuated, and he knew it. I thought it was love, but honestly, it just fed my obsession for the next level man.

We broke up in the beginning of December, and by the end of December, I was pregnant, but I was not his. This was the story of my life. I was so consumed by my emotions and my misery when I wasn't with someone that I couldn't sit still and heal. I was on to the next. It was a shame, but it was what my life had become. This first beautiful baby girl was just the beginning. My hunt for "love" was still on, and the depression had not gotten better. Before my daughter's first birthday, I was pregnant again. Every other year after that, I was having a new baby. You would have thought that I would have learned, but I had not. With every pregnancy, my depression became worse.

There would be days that I would lock up in the house and no one would even know that I was alive. The only reason that my mother would be able to get in was because she had a key. Shades closed, doors locked, cell phone ignored, and hibernation was the order of most of my days. I loved my children but honestly, I did not deserve to have them at the time. I was so sick that I lost, at least, 30 lbs. at the beginning of every pregnancy. I didn't learn. This happened five times. My first five children were out of wedlock. I wasn't just a promiscuous woman; I was a sexually addicted woman who suffered with severe depression, yet still loved God. This abnormal life had become my normal and I didn't know how to change it.

Overcoming Self

In one of my books entitled, *From Trash To Treasure: A Testimony of Hopelessness, Homelessness and Deliverance,* I tell the story of how my life really began to take a turn for the better. The relationship I found myself in about five years ago was one that led me down a road that I never thought I would come to. It started off as one heck of a love story as far as connections were concerned. We meshed like peanut butter and jelly on that brown bag, Captain Derst, yellow bread. It was sweet, and when we were together, there was no pressure to perform. All we had to do was just BE. However, I walked into this relationship with my eyes wide open to a few things that should have been a "no-no" for me from the very start, and they would have been had I had a standard for myself. The connection was great, but the extra bags that were attached to him were a million caution signs flashing "NO MA'AM!"

Needless to say, it all turned out to be a big trap to rip my heart to pieces. The thing is, I was just out of another relationship that was not very accepted by most of the people in my life. Most of the time, I was very happy, but it was not okay. No matter what others thought, however, the break up was tough, and it, of course, sent me into another heavy bout of depression. I had given up my apartment and everything to move out of town. The break up brought me back home sleeping on my mother's sofa with four kids in tow. It was more embarrassing to be back home after all the "I-told-you-so's." This was my normal, right? Instability was my self-appointed portion.

One thing was true, however. I still had my faith. Even in my sin, I had faith enough to pray and call on the Lord. I was a mess, but I knew that I was called to do something major in God's kingdom. I was prophetic, so I was very drawn to that life. I was still getting on prayer calls and even had an inspirational radio broadcast of my own. I was not so bold that I was calling it a prayer call. I was a preacher/prophet hiding behind the title of a motivational speaker. By this time, I was a certified life coach and an award-winning speaker, but I knew that God wanted more. The tearing apart of that relationship should have led me running back into God's embrace. Instead, it led me to Parker's gas station where I met the father of my fifth child. The one with the bags and the million flashing signs.

The realistic view would be that he was just a rebound dude. My reality was that he was "the one", and he would make it all better. He did for a minute. This was just more sin added on top of sin. Another baby came out of it, and, oh yeah, so did two years of homelessness.

In the book, however, I speak of this time of homelessness, and it was God's way of delivering me from myself and delivering me from the lie that I had convinced myself of. He was rescuing me, and for some reason, I knew that it was vitally important that I take heed this time. I did indeed.

I was saved before but living a life of no compromise started for me back in the year of 2013. This is the year that motivational speaking was not it anymore, and the full-time ministry that I was called to in 2010 had to come to full manifestation. For me, it was like a catching up of time that I lost. God was training me to be intentional and consistent in Him. He put me in a position where I could not have a man over at the house even if I wanted to because it was not allowed. But, I was ready this time. I was being thrown all types of offers. I was asked to be a mistress. I was asked to wait for two years until one guy finished using the other woman that he was with. Yes, he really asked me to do that. I was approached by men that I would have jumped on in a heartbeat just to cover up my hurt, but I was determined. God had been too good to me, and despite all that I thought I was because of my past, He saw me different.

Don't get me wrong; this was one of the toughest times in my life. I had tried being celibate before, and I had always made it only so far. The truth is that I have always loved God, I just didn't really love me enough to say no. I loved Him but my flesh only knew how to "cope" with the hurt and depression by getting my "fix." This go around, there was no turning back. There were nights that I was not just going through withdrawal symptoms, but I would lie in bed rocking myself and crying because my pit was so deep. I had to cry through it and even find a place, at times, to scream through it. Difficult was too soft a word for what this was for me. No matter how many times I heard someone preach the message, "God will keep those in perfect peace whose mind stays on Him," it did not make it better. My mind was on Him, but I was still craving sex to ease the state of depression, and I was getting more depressed because I felt that I was too weak to stay saved.

Being saved, chosen by God and called to preach the gospel did not make me exempt from the traps that were set for Creation. The enemy had set me up good fashion, and had I not chosen to fight to overcome myself, I would still be in that same pit today.

Understanding This Walk I'm On

There is much to understand about my mental "situation" and all that it brought along with it. Severe depression, I believe, was generational. It was a part of seed that was planted in an ancestor of mine long ago. I do not know how far back this struggle goes, but I know that it must not have been broken before me. Do I believe that mental health issues and mental illnesses are spiritual issues? Yes, I do. But, I believe that they are so ancient that to think that they can just be waved away is a myth. I honestly believe that to deal with this, we, as believers, must get really real with ourselves and take ownership. Deliverance needed to take place for me. God took me through it, but what I didn't understand was that even after deliverance, a renewed mind had to follow as well.

I was able to maintain because I had a strong determination not to grieve God anymore. Love was something that came from a pure heart, and it was relayed in action. During the maintaining, however, I was still struggling to focus on having a mindset that would change me totally. My thought was that I just needed to maintain until marriage. My mindset should have been on being totally and completely used by God and nothing more. See, though I was living without willfully sinning, my soul was still attached to men. I still craved them, and therefore, not having one was still my undoing.

In all that God was doing in me, I still had so much to learn, to fully understand the walk that I was on. I was on a journey to be free of all things that had me bound. I thought that I was doing it. I thought that I was free until I got married and got pregnant for the sixth time. Over the course of time, I was still dealing with big bouts of depression. I suffered with it for so many years that I don't think I truly knew what genuine joy was outside of the moment when I held my babies and nursed them. This last round with depression was so bad that I checked myself in the psychiatric hospital.

There were times when I would start to feel down out of the blue. Nothing had to happen to me or around me, it would just fall on me. Pregnancy times were always like 50 times worse however. I was married now, though, so why was I still so depressed? I thought that I always felt this way because I was so dirty, because I was touched inappropriately, because I was so loose. Being married should have made it all better, right? Nope, not even close. See, I had yet to look at this thing as the real issue, a real illness and spiritual battle. This last time truly opened my eyes.

Those ten days in the hospital did more to help me understand my walk with God and my battle than I ever had before. Now, I had been through deliverance. I had been cleansed, and I had worked through forgiving the people who had hurt me and tainted me. I also had been coached and even learned how to coach myself. During this time, however, God spoke so clearly to me. He allowed me the first two days to sleep, to rest. He began to speak, "Shalonda, you have been delivered, but your mind has not been renewed. You know how to praise me, you come before me truly wanting to be cleansed, but after you have poured out, you go back to settling into those times when you are in your pit. You scream about how no one gets you and how they never will. You rest in your weaknesses instead of being aware of the weak place and working towards strengthening it. I allowed you to come here to renew your mind and to get unstuck."

That was so interesting to me. Most people in the church and in ministry would say that once you have gone through deliverance, that it is enough. Romans 12:2 says, "that we must be transformed by the renewing of our minds." I didn't know my triggers. I was not mindful of how my thoughts would begin to race at certain moments and how the enemy would use my triggers to get back in a place of defeat, so that I would be of no use to the kingdom. Since that time, I have yet to have a critical moment, better yet, a week or some months, of depression. After 30 years of spending more time down in my soul than up, I would say that this is cause for a great celebration.

Snatching my soul back

When I refer to my soul, I am referring to what we know as our mind. This is the center of us. It is what we think with, choose with and feel with. So, when you hear the words, "He sold his soul to the devil," it is speaking to the fact that someone has given up his freedom to choose for himself, and he is now allowing the evil one to choose for him.

I did not realize it "back in the day," but the enemy had taken my soul, and it had been dominated by depression and controlled by who liked me and who did not and what I could give in return for being accepted. My spirit was willing to be better, but my flesh was weak and what was on my mind, more often than not, won out. My soul had been snatched, but I was determined to snatch it right back.

As I preach and teach thousands and thousands of people across the world how to grow closer to God, I don't claim to be perfect nor do I claim that depression doesn't try to creep up. The thing that you have been set free from will always try you to see if it can find a way back in. I will say that my determination gets stronger and stronger every day to submit to God and resist the devil so that he can keep fleeing from me. Depression is not my portion. I used to take many medicines for it, and there are times where if I truly need to, I will. For almost two years now, since I snatched my soul back from the enemy, I have not had to take any and my joy has been overflowing.

Everybody has a different story. I do not claim to have the answer for all of them. What I do know is that God is real, and so is freedom. I wanted mine so badly and to have my soul back after 30 years of being oppressed feels like heaven to me. Selah.

Molestation, Promiscuity, and Sexual Addiction

Demetria Hill Cannady, PhD, LPC

Molest is defined as to make annoying sexual advances to; to force physical and usually sexual contact on (www.merriam-webster.com). **Molestation** as defined by *"The Free Dictionary,"* is the crime of sexual acts with children up to the age of 18-years-old, including touching of private parts, exposure to genitalia, taking of pornographic pictures, rape, inducement of sexual acts with the molester or other children, and variations of these acts by pedophiles. Molestation also applies to incest by a relative with a minor family member, and any unwanted sexual acts with adults' short of rape. **Rape** is the unlawful sexual activity and usually sexual intercourse carried out forcibly or under threat of injury against the will usually of a female or with a person who is beneath a certain age or incapable of valid consent (www.merrriam-webster.com). **Statutory rape** is sexual intercourse by an adult with a person below a statutorily designated age. The criminal offense is committed when an adult sexually penetrates a person who under the law, is incapable of consenting to sex under rape statutes in all states. These persons are considered deserving of special protection because they are especially vulnerable due to their youth or condition (www.legaldictionary.thefreedictionary.com).

Promiscuous is having or characterized by many transient sexual relationships; demonstrating or implying an undiscriminating or unselective approach; indiscriminate or casual (www.dictionary.com). **Sexual addiction (nymphomania, hypersexuality, satyriasis, erotomania, compulsive sexual behaviors, Don Juanism, and Don Juanitaism)** is a term used to describe a person that feels a lack of control or restraint concerning their sexual thoughts, urges, and behaviors. Compulsive sexual thoughts and acts alongside difficulties with intimacy. Some of the sex acts associated with sexual addiction are watching pornography, masturbation, phone sex, cybersex, escorts, prostitution, extramarital affairs, attending strip clubs, voyeurism, and exhibitionism (www.addictions.com).

WHAT HAPPENS IN THIS HOUSE, THIS HOUSE......STAYS IN

African American families have a long-standing history of family secrets. As children, most of us have been told what happens in this house stays in this house. Often that which happened in the house was something that hurt, something we feared, and/or caused us shame so much so that we would not want to share. Topics which we dared not discuss were: molestation, physical abuse, verbal abuse, sexual abuse, alcoholism, drug abuse, homosexuality, illegitimate children, and mental health issues. Many family secrets have hindered growth in individuals as well as caused division amongst family members. Often due to the unspoken hurts, the hurts continue from one generation to another. For example: "Uncle Joe" molested my mother, molested me, and will molest my daughter if we continue to say nothing. However, when I decide to speak, the family becomes upset with me and accuses me of being a liar because no one before me disclosed their hurts. Even as I share my pain, my mother continues to sit silent as not to be ridiculed by the rest of the family. She leaves me to be slaughtered by everyone else. However, in secret conversations amongst one another, we disclose and support one another, but when it comes to public justice, I stand alone. We live what we learn, positive and negative. We also try to run away from the truth, most times not successfully.

In working in the mental health field, as therapists, we encounter many women who were molested as children. Sometimes to manage the lack of control that they had over their bodies (after being victimized) as children and/or teenagers, the individuals became promiscuous because they felt they had control if they gave their body away instead of being taken advantage of by someone. Some individuals enjoyed the attention they received from the older boys/men which also led them down the road of promiscuity. In their minds, any attention received was deemed "good attention" when in fact, being taken advantage of sexually was not good attention. One in four women have been sexually abused as children. When children tried to share their experience of being violated, they were called a liar by family and friends or told, "You wanted it;" "It was your fault;" or "You were being fast." Family/friends made the victim feel ashamed, embarrassed, or at fault so the victim became silent, thus holding in their pain, acting out in other ways. Abused children have been unable to live their truth of being molested and have been "tricked," "threatened," and "subjected" to silence, by the family, especially if the predator was a family member or a friend of the family.

People attend church as a means of healing but find themselves ostracized in church as well if church members know of or suspect an individual to be a survivor of molestation, rape, or sexual abuse. Hypothetically speaking, a church which has 200 members (100 men and 100 women) will have at least forty-one child abuse survivors (20.5%). In some instances, the pastors are unable to help the victim heal because they too are victims themselves and have not healed their past hurts. In other instances, the pastors have been deemed the predator, "preying," on the victim thus causing further confusion and pain.

Interestingly, sexual offenders, whether family or strangers, describe themselves as "religious." Offenders voiced that "church people" are easy to fool because Christians are so trusting. Research shared that there are many people in the church who are suffering from sexual addiction. In addition, more than 80% of women who have a porn addiction will advance their addiction, thus acting out their behaviors in "real life." Molestation advances to promiscuity and promiscuity advances to sexual addiction, and sex is used to fill the void because of the molestation and/or sexual abuse.

References

Molest, 2017. Retrieved from: https://www.merriam-webster.com.

Molestation, 2017. Retrieved from: https://www.freedictionary.com.

Promiscuous, 2017. Retrieved from: https://www.dictionary.com.

Rape, 2017. Retrieved from: https://www.merriam-webster.com.

Sexual Addiction, 2017. Retrieved from: https://www.addictions.com.

Statutory Rape, 201). Retrieved from: https://www.legaldictionary.thefreedictioanry.com.

Minister Melinee Calhoun, PhD is an active member of Gateway to Heaven United Holiness Church, Inc. in Lakeland, Georgia. She is the divorced mother of two daughters. Minister Calhoun graduated from Valdosta Technical with certificate in First Aid & Safety and as a Certified Customer Service Specialist in 2000, in 2005. She graduated from Valdosta State University with a BA in Criminal Justice and went on to receive her Master Degree in Business Administration from Liberty University in 2006 and a PhD in Public Policy and Administration/Criminal Justice from Walden University in 2016.

She is an avid poet and enjoys spoken word. Currently, she works as a Community Supervision Officer (felony probation and parole) with the State of Georgia Department of Community Supervision. Her life's mission is to push people and challenge others work daily at being a better person day by day as well as to instill others with the knowledge, skills and abilities to be assets to society rather than liabilities. "My life's worth is assessed by the impact I have on others around me."

Contact Information:

Melineecalhoun@yahoo.com

(229) 506-2692- Phone

@juztiphied (Twitter/Instagram)

Journey to Me

Minister Melinee Calhoun, PhD, MBA

Life is a journey. Treasure hunt of sorts. Some seek lavishness, riches and fame. Some seek that which in minute in the eyes of others. My lost treasure was in fact, me. We lose ourselves in our relationships with others. We lose ourselves in search of ourselves. At the end of the day, I must seek the face of God in order to save me from me. Who am I? Where am I? Where am I going? From whence did I come? Lost in a world of chaos. Looking over into an abyss of nothingness. How do I get from this place? A lack of self-worth, a lack of self-knowledge, a lack of self-love for years fed the emptiness inside me. The emptiness that if uncontrolled will continue growing and spreading and create a chasm which pushes me further and further away from myself. Seeing myself in the distance, I yearn to belong, I yearn to be connected, I yearn to be accepted. I'm torn into pieces: spiritually, mentally, and emotionally.

What can make me whole? What can free me from the chains that bind my sanity? What can save me from losing me and yet save me from myself? All are questions that have haunted me for years. From a young age, I knew I was different. I knew there was a call, a purpose, a plan, a divine design, yet that didn't stop me from kicking against the prick as I aged. I didn't want to be different, I wanted to fit in. I didn't want to stand out, I wanted to blend in. As I grew into my older teenage years, my mentality shifted momentarily, but as I became an adult I fell back into that desires to be as one in the world. I battled with myself. I battled against myself. I fought many times trying to be what I was not and this in fact caused me to experience many heartaches and pains. Thru it all, the real "ME" shall prevail.

My mother and father were both teenagers when they began to minister the Word of God, so well before I was conceived, they were on the battlefield. My mother in fact went into labor with me while in a midnight service. From that day to this, the enemy has pursued me with a vengeance. Even from a young age, the enemy tried to stop me before I could grow into adulthood. This is why I know there is a plan and purpose for my life and it must be fulfilled. At the tender age of one or so, while on a fishing creek with my parent and their friends, I jumped into the dark, murky water after a fishing cork. My father was on the other side of the creek and my mother didn't know how to swim. But for a mother's love, she blindly jumped in after me, pulling me up being covered in mud and weeds. That was the first of many battles that I still this day must continue to fight. As I grew older, looking back it was one of the many times the enemy tried to take me out. At some point between the ages of two and three, I snuck outside, and I climbed up a standing ladder that was propped up on my parents' home. After reaching the top, I walked around the roof, pulling off my clothing and undergarments. My parents searched frantically trying to find me, until a neighbor happened to see me walking around on the roof. Oh, the possibilities!

From my entrance into head start until the day I graduated high school, I was bullied at every turn. I'd come home and cry, only wanting the torment to end. Unfortunately, during that day and time, society was not as well-versed on the impacts and effects of bullying, so my parents were not properly educated in dealing with bullying and their best advice was to pray about it, stay close to the teacher, and let someone know if something happens. Unfortunately, in my mind, prayer was not working, "tattle-telling" was only going to make it worse, and there were times in which no adult was within the immediate vicinity to help me. What was I to do? I cried and prayed and prayed and cried the more. I even tried to pay the bullies to leave me alone. Just imagine; you're a 9-year-old in the 4th grade, and you're taking money from home just to pay your bullies to leave you alone. I cried for God to just let me die. In my mind's eye, death was easier. Even the thought of suicide was hard for my mother to fathom. Though they may not have known how to effectively eliminate the issue from a natural respect, I know that war was abounding in the spiritual realm.

With the spiritual war that was raging, the natural battles that I had to face were persistent, as the enemy had it in for me. While nine years of age, I was swimming at the river with my family, I jumped into a sinkhole from which my father saved me. At nineteen years old, just four weeks after giving birth to my oldest child, I was hit by a speeding driver coming down a four-lane highway. He told the officers that he was so scared because it was déjà vu in that the year prior, he had hit someone, and the person died. After being taken to the ER, I had no broken bones and one scratch on the palm of my hand from the impact of crushing the glass of his windshield. The devil thought he had me that day. You always hear people talk about their lives flashing before their eyes, but many people don't experience it and live to speak about it. This was certainly one occasion in which my life flashed before my eyes in slow motion. I remember crossing the street in a rage of anger and not paying attention to traffic. When the car hit me, I did not even see it coming. I remember the impact of the car as I saw myself "flying through the air." As I came tumbling to the ground, I first landed on the windshield of the car, crushing it. I rolled to the ground, and it was as if the hand of God stopped the vehicle just in time before the tires of the vehicle could run me over. There are many witnesses to this miracle as there were at least one hundred people gathered at this well-known nightclub called "Brandy's" on Hill Avenue in Valdosta, GA. I had no business there and was only there because the guy I was dating was there with another woman, and I was there to confront him. The devil *thought* he had me. The enemy sought my life that night, BUT GOD!

At the age of twenty, I was diagnosed with thyroid cancer. The doctor refused to see me at first, saying that I was too young to have an issue with my thyroid and that she only sees patients over twenty-five years old. At the persistence of my mother and the referral from another doctor, the endocrinologist had no choice but to see me. She told me I'd never have any more children; I'd likely be infertile, but in 2006, I birthed a second child. In 2003, while working at KFC, I began having severe pains in my abdomen. I worked through it. The next day I went to school at VSU and was so sick, I rode over an hour on the transit not wanting to move. Eventually, I went to the school infirmary, and I was given Pepto Bismol to take. The Pepto Bismol did nothing. I went home and eventually my mother took me to the ER. They took various test and scans, but the hospital in Lakeland, GA did not employ a physician that could read the scans. The scans were sent to South Georgia Medical Center, SGMC, where they were placed on the doctor's desk and not looked at for hours. After several hours, the ER staff called SGMC to inquire about the scans. Upon looking at the scans, the physician called the ER and at 3 AM, I was rushed into surgery as my appendix was on the verge of rupturing. Doctors later said that if it had been one hour later, my appendix would have ruptured...BUT GOD!

As the years passed by, God began to reveal more of His plan and purpose in my life. I knew at a young age that there was a work for me to do, and I fought against it for years. By August of 2012, I'd come to accept God's plan and completed my trial sermon under the leadership of Bishop and Pastor Calhoun of Gateway to Heaven United Holiness Church, Inc. My subject was titled "Is you is or is you ain't: Cause you can't make it faking." Many people get caught up in the spiritual gray area, and they straddle the fence, but God does not want half of us. He wants it all or nothing. As I began to grow in my faith, I was of the impression that my spiritual walk and my relationship with God would keep me from having so many battles; BOY WAS I WRONG! Little did I know that the battles had just begun. As time continued to pass, I found myself in a domestic violence situation. I was scared for my life and contemplated suicide as my way out. I even contemplated homicide as a means to an end. Can you imagine what went through my mind when the day came that I was beaten because I was praying? The enemy thought that it would cause me to question God and to lose faith in God. I felt like I had been beaten for my belief, and admittedly, I did ask God "why me?" I did not understand, but one day, God reminded me of the scripture *"...rejoicing that they were counted worthy to suffer shame for his name"* (Acts 5:41, KJV). Even in the midst of my suffering, God had shown favor, and I bless him daily for those life experiences and learning lessons. Time and time again, I've lost myself in love or now looking back, it would best be classified as lust. The price I've paid for kicking against the prick.

Many would say that if they could go back in the past with the knowledge they have now, then their life would be completely different. Though this is likely true, I prefer to live by the principle that everything I've experienced in life has played an integral role in shaping, molding and making me. We use the cliché, "When life hands you lemons, make lemonade," but I rather like the concept taught to me by my father [Bishop Otis Lee Calhoun]. Being an automotive mechanic by trade, he likened life experiences to a car battery. A car battery has both negative and positive posts. If you remove the positive post and try to crank the vehicle, it will not crank up. If you remove the negative post, and place the positive back on, it yet and still will not crank.

Only when you have both positive and negative posts properly connected and tightened will the car crank up. The same goes with life; our negative experiences impact us just as much as the positive one. The negative experiences are just as influential and needed as the positive. Many times, we wish to rid ourselves of the negative, but we would not be who we are without them. My life experiences were all a positive force in my life, so I have learned not to classify my "so called" "negative" experiences as negative. Why? Were they a detriment to my life or did they have a lasting negative impact on my life? NO! Those experiences were a positive driving force in my life that were allowed and ordained by God. I give no credit or power to the enemy in anything that I have experienced because God allowed it, and He allowed it for a reason.

As a child, I found myself feeling alone, and I found comfort and solace in the company of my stuffed animals. I remember having dozens of them, and I'd line them up on a stand in my room and pretend they were a choir, and I was the director. As I grew older, I developed a love for reading, but unlike others, I didn't want to read regular fiction or nonfiction books; rather I chose to read the dictionary. To this day, the dictionary is my favorite book. By the 9th grade, I told my mother that I needed a new dictionary as I had read all the words in the one I owned. Words and wordplay became my passion. When I was 8 years old, I told my parents that God had called me to preach. As I grew older, I began to craft these eloquently written sermons. I remember getting an allowance of $5-10, and without fail, I gladly paid my 10%. Being a child and knowing you're different is difficult so I battled with myself. I wanted to be like everyone else. The more I tried to be like others, the greater the distance I created with myself. I began to think that if I were more like them, then the bullying would stop. As to be expected, it only got worse.

After entering high school, I completed my 9th grade year and I set it in my mind that I was going to show them [the bullies]. I did nothing but study. Studying became a lifestyle for me. Education became a motivator. My thirst for the acquisition of more knowledge was and is ever abounding. The more they bullied, the harder I studied. From being called, "Celie," to the "Predator," nothing was going to stop me from achieving my mission. My studies paid off in many ways, as my science teacher took attention to my aptitude and enrolled me into the National and International Chemistry Olympiad. I was the first person from my school to ever participate in the competition. Later, she gave me the chemistry book from her class, saying it needed to be retired.

Throughout my high school career, I consistently ranked 1st, 2nd or 3rd for the academic year. My senior year, I received more awards/recognitions than anyone else in my class. At graduation, I was the only African American student to graduate with honors. I went on to be the first person in my immediate family to graduate from a four-year college; the only one to have a master's degree, and/or a PhD. It was not me though. It had nothing to do with me. It was the God that lives in me.

Through all my successes and failures, I continue to ebb and flow in my efforts to find myself. Throughout my childhood and adulthood, I've experienced various gifts of God. One of which I've hated much of my life. In my dreams, I see foresee death. As my relationship with God grew, and I came closer to finding myself, my gift was heightened. I began to see clearer. Being a young child, this was quite frightening, and even as an adult, I fear it at times. As I lose a sense of myself, my gift is weakened. At a peak in my gift, on one Saturday in December 2012, I dreamed of my mother lying in a casket. Mind you, I don't dream of death in this manner generally, but my dreams are interpreted as death. This dream of my mother must mean something else. I went to my father to ask him, and before I could ask him, something happened, and he was called away. I never got the opportunity to ask him about the dream, but exactly one week later, my dream became a reality. After my mother took her last breath, I couldn't find any other words, but Thank You Lord. I began to bless the name of God in the midst of my trial and tribulations. The peace that He gave me surpasses all understanding. My mother passed to me a baton and light that I must forever wave high. I've wavered and faulted along the way, and slowly but surely, I've found my way.

I have learned so many lucrative lessons throughout the experiences in my life, both natural and spiritual. Two of the most important, impactful and powerful lessons that I have learned are

1) if the enemy is not fighting me, then I must not be on the right road or on the right path; and 2) if my words are so powerful which lends my tongue to be an untamable beast, then the Word of God is most definitely infinite in power, so in all things I should speak life and declare the Word of God.

First, as mentioned, if the enemy is not bothering you, he likely has you where he wants you, so there is no need of him to bother you. The enemy knows that if he fights you, then you are more apt to run to and seek God for direction, guidance and help. So, why would he bother you when he has you where he wants you? When the enemy is fighting you tooth and nail, that is when you know you are in the right direction. The closer I get to God and the stronger my relationship is with God, the more the enemy fights me. Consider Job, the Bible tells us that Job was a perfect man, and the enemy indeed sought to make Job curse God. The battles endured by Job were in fact because of the relationship that Job had with God, and the enemy wanted to destroy that relationship. At the end of the day, this journey is not about us. The enemy is not really concerned with you, but rather he is only concerned with God. How better to hurt God than to bother His children or to cause His creation to turn their backs on Him? Thus why, the enemy does not fight you when he knows you already in his corner; though that is not to say that he does not seek to destroy you while in the midst of your sins. Some people might question why then do non-believers suffer if the enemy is not fighting them, and the fact of the matter is that many times trials and tribulations come by the hand of God, for the purpose of causing them to turn to Him.

Secondly, and more importantly, the power in words is exponential. We must be mindful not to speak damnation and death in our lives, and in the varied situations in which we find ourselves involved. It is of the utmost importance to speak life in everything. If the words that proceed from my lips have so much power, then without a shadow of doubt, I know that the Word of God is power without borders. I cannot even begin to imagine the extent of the power in the Word of God. I have learned to speak the Word of God in every situation. I imagine that I am not the only person to have ever experienced someone throwing my words back at me, as to say, "This is what you said, and I expect you to be a woman of your word." Throughout my experiences I have learned to go to God and say:

"Lord, you said in your Word, not my word, but your Word that you would never leave or forsake. You said, ask...seek...knock (Matthew 7:7, KJV). You said, seek your Kingdom and everything else would be given to me (Matthew 6:33, KJV). You said to speak those things that are not as though they were (Romans 4:17, KJV). You said that I have not because I ask not (James 4:2, KJV). You said that with faith the size of a mustard size that mountains could be moved (Matthew 17:20, KJV). You said that all things are possible, if I only believe (Mark 9:23, KJV). You said the wicked's wealth was awaiting the righteous (Proverbs 13:22, KJV). You said, the animals, forest and cattle [on a thousand hills] were yours (Psalms 50:10). I believe that even the hill itself is yours. You said for me to come boldly to your throne of grace (Hebrew 4:16, KJV). Lord, you said, "God is not a man, that he should lie; neither the son of man, that he should repent: hath He said, and shall He not do it? or hath He spoken, and shall He not make it good" (Number 23:19, KJV). Lord you said it, therefore, I speak it, I declare it, I decree it and it is so.

Regardless of what life may present, it is essential that we remain rooted and grounded in the Word of God. The Word of God never fails, so if I am in the God and His Word is in me, then I shall never fail.

Instilled within me are the values, principles and the drive of a Proverbs 31 woman. I seek the face of God Almighty daily. For He is my Jehovah Jireh! In Him, do I live and breathe. He alone is worthy. My journey in search of me is a path that God designed for me, and though I diverted on numerous occasions, my path always leads me back to my humble beginning. God kept me for a reason, a season, and a divine design. Many times, the enemy thought he had me, but God said, not so. I shall run my course, I shall finish this race and when all is said and done, I will hear Him say, 'Well done'.

BULLYING
Demetria Hill Cannady, PhD, LPC

Bully is the use of superior strength or influence to intimidate (someone), typically to force him or her to do what one wants (wisegeek.org). Bullying is an unwanted, aggressive behavior among school aged children that involves a real or perceived imbalance of power. The behaviors are repeated or has the potential to be repeated (www.stopbullying.com). It used to be that term bullying was associated with children and in childhood. However, bullying has become prominent within the adult population as well. Adult bullies are not as overt as the children bullies. Adult bullies are crafty when they are bullying others and do so mainly with verbal bullying. Many may dismiss bullying behaviors because the bullies ensure that they are not targeting the victims for others to see. Adult bullying has become common as much as the childhood bullying.

There are four forms of bullying: physical, verbal, social, and cyber bullying. **Physical bullying** hurts someone's body or damages their possessions. Stealing, shoving, hitting, fighting, and destroying property. Physical bullying is rarely the first form of bullying. **Verbal bullying** is a means of using words in a negative way such as insults, teasing, put downs, threats of harm, and inappropriate sexual comments; and to gain power over someone's life. Verbal bullying has destroyed many lives at home, school, and in business settings. **Social bullying** involves spreading rumors about another person, purposely leaving someone out of an activity or group or embarrassing a person in public. **Cyber bullying** is the use of electronic communications to bully a person, typically by sending messages of intimidating or threatening (www.wisegeek.org).

An individual, child or adult, who has been bullied tends to have poor self-image, low self-esteem, and little to no self-worth. Self-image is the idea one has about her abilities, appearance, and personality; how you perceive yourself. Self-esteem is respect or favorable image of oneself (www.randomhousedictionary.com). The evaluative, attitudinal component of the self; the affective judgments placed on the self-concept. Self-esteem consists of feelings of worth and acceptance and develops because of a sense of identity, awareness of competence, and feedback from the external world (The Counseling Dictionary). Self-worth is the sense of one's own value or worth as a person; self-esteem; self-respect (www.dictionary.com); a feeling that you are a good person who deserves to be treated with respect (www.merriam-webster.com). Being bullied damages an individual mentally long-term; they don't get over being bullied in a year or two. Some individuals have the trauma associated with bullying for decades.

Numerous people have been bullied as children. Kids who are bullied and who bully others may have problems which continue into adulthood. Those bullying behaviors experienced as a child could manifest in the form of low self-esteem, poor self-image/self-worth, anger issues. Low self-esteem and low self-worth can often lead women allowing themselves to be made to feel "less than" by others, allowing others to misuse them, and allowing others to emotionally, verbally, physically, and sexually abuse them. On the other hand, the individual may take the opposite approach and the bullying becomes the "fuel of the fire" to overcome the negative words spoken/actions taken which were meant to break you and your spirit. When we were children bullying was simpler and came in the form of verbal abuse (primarily name calling) and physical abuse (shoving, pinching, hitting, and kicking) but this date and time bullying has taken on new dimensions. These new dimensions include social bullying and cyber bullying. "Mean-Girls" take on a whole new meaning because they take their bullying to an elevated level to include social media. The expression "hurt people will hurt people," reigns true with the new forms of bullying whether it is meant to keep you out a social circle or extremes such as damaging marriages and careers.

In completing research for this project, I came across several types of adult bullies: Narcissistic Adult Bully; Impulsive Adult Bully; Physical Bully; Verbal Adult Bully; Secondary Adult Bully: and Workplace Bully. "**Narcissistic Adult Bullies** are self-centered and do not share empathy with others. They possess very little anxiety about consequences. This type of bully appears to feel good about themselves, but, has a brittle narcissism that requires them to put others down. **Impulsive Adult Bullies** are more spontaneous and do not really plan their bullying. This type of bully has little self-restraint and sometimes their bullying is not intentional which results in them feeling stressed, upset, or concerned about a situation which may have nothing to do with the victim. **Physical Bullies** use physical confrontation. They may not actually harm the victim but will use threats of harm or physical domination through threatening. A physical bully may damage or steal the victim's property rather than physically confronting the victim," (www.bullyingstatistics.org).

"**Verbal Adult Bullies** use words that may be damaging; they start rumors about the victim or use sarcastic or demeaning language to dominate or humiliate another person. This type of bullying is difficult to document but has emotional and psychological effects. Verbal bullying can also cause depression or poor job performance at the job and in the home environment. **Secondary Adult Bullies** is the individual who accompanies the bully in their bullying behaviors. In addition, this individual may feel bad about assisting the bully but is ensuring and securing the loyalty of the bully so that he/she does not become a victim later. **Workplace Bullying** takes place in the work environment making life difficult, especially work life. These bullies make life miserable, disrupt productivity, create a hostile work environment, and reduce the morale of their co-workers. They have a pattern and are interested in power and domination; they want to be the preferred staff member and feel important. Workplace bullies will put others work down to make their work appear more superior. These individuals also put the company in jeopardy of a lawsuit," (www.bullyingstatistics.org).

In a therapeutic setting, we have individuals who come in on a regular basis who have been victims of bullying and experienced bullying as children. Sometimes bullying is the traumatic event which has kept them "stuck" as a child and most often as an adult. When speaking with individuals about having been bullied, they can vividly remember the event as though it happened the day before. Based on their physical and verbal responses, you can know whether they have overcome the trauma of the event or this is where they're "stuck" and require interventions to address trauma. As therapists, we have the tools and interventions needed to assist the individual to move past the traumatic event and possibly forgive the individual(s) who has caused them so much emotional pain.

However, as ministers and spiritual leaders, these individuals are members of your congregation, and while they may be one of your best church members and participants, they are still existing in the spirit of unforgiveness. In addition to therapy to address bullying, they will need and require your assistance in providing them with scriptures and spiritual tools to assist them with moving forward with their lives by practicing forgiveness. Thus, explaining that forgiveness is for them more so than for the individual whom they need to forgive. Forgiveness frees up the blessing that may have been previously hindered due to being in a state of bitterness, resentment, and unforgiveness for the person who caused them hurt and harm.

References:

Cyber Bullying, 2017. Retrieved from: https://www.wisegeek.org.

Impulsive Adult Bullying, 2017. Retrieved from https://www.bullyingstatistics.org.

Narcissistic Adult Bullying, 2017. Retrieved from https://www.bullyingstatistics.org.

Physical (Adult) Bullying, 2017. Retrieved from https://www.bullyingstatistics.org.

Physical Bullying, 2017. Retrieved from: https://www.wisegeek.org.

Secondary Adult Bullying, 2017. Retrieved from https://www.bullyingstatistics.org.

Self-Esteem, 2017. Retrieved from: https://www.thecounselingdictionary.com.

Self-Esteem, 2017. Retrieved from: https://www.randomhousedictionary.com

Self-Worth, 2017. Retrieved from: https://www.dictionary.com.

Self-Worth, 2017. Retrieved from: https://www.meeriam-webster.com.

Social Bullying, 2017. Retrieved from: https://www.wisegeek.org.

Verbal (Adult) Bullying, 2017. Retrieved from https://www.bullyingstatistics.org.

Verbal Bullying, 2017. Retrieved from: https://www.wisegeek.org.

Workplace Bullying, 2017. Retrieved from https://www.bullyingstatistics.org.

Domestic Violence

Demetria Hill Cannady, PhD, LPC

I have often heard women say, "He didn't mean to hit me. He was just angry;" "He says he hits me because he loves me;" "I shouldn't have made him angry. I shouldn't have talked back, etc." Ladies if he hits you, that IS NOT love. That is a man that needs help, an intervention, whether it is anger management, jail time, or an end to the relationship with you alive. The National Coalition Against Domestic Violence defines Domestic Violence as the "willful intimidation, physical assault, battery, sexual assault, and/or other abusive behavior as part of a systematic pattern of power and control perpetrated by one intimate partner against another. It includes physical violence, sexual violence, psychological violence, and emotional abuse. It is described as epidemic which is affecting individuals in every community, regardless of age, economic status, sexual orientation, gender, race, religion, or nationality. Most perpetrators are law-abiding citizens outside the home environment. Domestic violence situations/relationships can have the result of an individual sustaining a physical injury, psychological trauma, and even death," (www.ncadv.org). Domestic Violence not only affects the individual victim and/or perpetrator; it affects the family members, immediate and extended. The trauma can be felt inter-generationally because it affects the children, parents, and grandparents, especially if the domestic violence ended with a death occurring.

There are several types of Domestic Violence situations: Intimate partner physical abuse; Psychological abuse; Economic abuse; Sexual assault; Stalking; Dating abuse and teen violence (to include college campuses); Male victims of intimate partner abuse; Domestic violence involving guns; Domestic violence among elders; Domestic violence with result being homicide (www.ncadv.org). Domestic Violence comes in the form of emotional, psychological, and physical violence and intensifies over time with the perpetrator becoming more aggressive and controlling over time. The perpetrator does not trust the victim, becomes "jealous, possessive, and becomes accusatory;" will call the victim inappropriate names making them feel less than; and they threaten to bring hurt/harm/kill the victim sometimes including the children and parents in these threats. Perpetrators of domestic violence will keep their victims in isolation and "away from family and friends; control finances; tell them victim what they can wear or not to wear; use intimidation; force the victim to have sex with him and/or his friends; and destroy the victim's property," (www.ncadv.org).

Most victims of domestic violence will minimize what they are experiencing within their relationship; will have low self-esteem and feel powerless; feel inadequate and do not recognize their value within their community; they will accept "stress, alcohol, and drugs" as the reason for the violence experienced. However, there are red flags that you may look for if you are a victim of domestic violence or feel that your friend or family member is in a domestic violence relationship. These include:

- Extreme jealousy
- Possessiveness
- Unpredictability
- Bad temper
- Cruelty to animals (look for this in young children also)
- Verbal abuse
- Extremely controlling behavior
- Antiquated beliefs about men/women relationship roles
- Forced sex
- Sabotage of birth control
- Blaming the victim for anything bad that happens
- Sabotage victim at school/work
- Control finances
- Abuse of other family members, children, or pets
- Accusations of flirting or infidelity
- Controls what the victim wears/acts
- Demeans the victim in public and in private
- Embarrassment or humiliation of victim in front of others
- Harassment of the victim at work

(www.ncadv.org)

Here are a few Domestic Violence Statistics via Domesticviolencestats.org which were updated in April 2017, so these facts and figures are current:

- Every 9 seconds in the US a woman is assaulted or beaten.

- Around the world, at least one in every three women has been beaten, coerced into sex or otherwise abused during her lifetime. Most often, the abuser is a member of her own family.

- Domestic violence is the leading cause of injury to women- more than car accidents, muggings, and rapes combined.

- Studies suggest that up to 10 million children witness some form of domestic violence annually.

- Nearly 1 in 5 teenage girls who have been in a relationship said a boyfriend threatened violence or self-harm if presented with a breakup.

- Every day in the US, more than three women are murdered by their husbands or boyfriends.

- Ninety-two percent of women surveyed listed reducing domestic violence and sexual assault as their top concern.

- Domestic violence victims lose nearly 8 million days of paid work per year in the US alone- the equivalent of 32,000 full-time jobs.

- Based on reports from 10 countries, between 55 percent and 95 percent of women who had been physically abused by their partners had never contacted non-governmental organizations, shelters, or the police for help.

- The costs of intimate partner violence in the US alone exceed $5.8 billion per year: $4.1 billion are for direct medical and health care services, while productivity losses account for nearly $1.8 billion.

- Men who as children witnessed their parents' domestic violence were twice as likely to abuse their own wives than sons of nonviolent parents.

In America, one woman is fatally shot by a spouse, ex-spouse, or dating partner every 14 hours and there are 433 domestic violence gun related fatalities which have occurred this year since 1/1/17. The Domestic Violence Hotline – 1-800-799-SAFE (7233) or www.TheHotline.org.

References:

National Coalition Against Domestic Violence (www.ncadv.org)
American Journal of Public Health, 104(3), 461-466, doi: 10.2105/AJPH.2013.301582.

National Coalition Against Domestic Violence (www.ncadv.org)
Black, M.C. Basile, K.C., Breiding, M.J., Smith, S.G., Walters, M.L., Merrick, M.T., Chen, J. & Stevens, M. (2011). *The national intimate partner and sexual violence survey:2010 summary report.* Retrieved from http://www.cdc.gov/violenceprevention/pdf/nisvs_report2010-a.pdf.

National Coalition Against Domestic Violence (www.ncadv.org)
Bridges, F.B., Tatum, K.M., & Kunselman, J.C. (2008). Domestic violence statutes and rates of intimate partner and family homicide: A research note. *Criminal Justice Policy Review, 19*(1), 117-130.

National Coalition Against Domestic Violence (www.ncadv.org)
Campbell, J.C., Webster, D., Koziol-McLain, J., Block, C., Campbell, D., Curry, M.A., Gary, F., Glass, N., McFarlane, J., Sachs, C. Sharps, P., Ulrich, Y., Wilt, S., Manganello, J., Xu, X. Schollenberger, J., Frye, V. & Lauphon, K. (2003). Risk factors for femicide in abusive relationships: Results from a multisite case control study. *American Journal of Public Health,* 93(7), 1089-1097.

National Coalition Against Domestic Violence (www.ncadv.org)
Truman, J.L. & Morgan, R.E. (2014). *Nonfatal domestic violence, 2003-2012.* Retrieved from http://www.bjs.gov/content/pub/pdf/ndv0312.pdf.

National Coalition Against Domestic Violence (www.ncadv.org)
World Health Organization (2013). *Global and regional estimates of violence against women: Prevalence and health effects of intimate partner violence and non-partner sexual violence.* Retrieved from https://apps.who.int/iris/bitstream/10665/85239 /1/9789241564625 _eng.pdf?ua=1.

Jan Glover is a therapist from Jacksonville, Florida who graduated from Jean Ribault Senior High School. While Jan attended Florida State University she became pregnant with her first and only child, Jyra Graham. However, she earned a Bachelor of Social Work Degree from Florida State University School of Social Work and a Master Degree in Family Therapy from Nova Southeastern University Nassau, and Bay counties.

Following her graduate studies her life changed. During her Air Force enlistment process at Moody Air Force Base her labs were abnormal due to carcinoid tumors. During the course of her treatment she had a full gastrectomy; leaving her cancer free but without a stomach. Although her road to recovery has been rough her desire to help others remains the same. Jan has grassroots, nonprofit organization, "Connecting the Dots of Jacksonville" which participates in community involvement, youth initiatives, writing development, book publishing, grant writing, and therapeutic services.

Contact Information:
Jan Glover. BSW, MS
Phone (904) 631-1520
ctdjax@gmail.com

HOW I GOT OVER
Jan Glover, BSW, MS

I have been given the task of exploring my spiritual journey and discussing my mental health along the way as a therapist. I am not ashamed of the gospel of Jesus Christ and all the great things he has done for me! At the age of 9 I was baptized in the formerly "New Mount Tabor Missionary Baptist Church" in Jacksonville, Florida where I continue to hold membership. Through faith I know that all things will continue to work out for my good. My two most extreme tests of that faith occurred in 1998 and 2010. I also had similar tests of faith in 1993 and 1995 but since I did not reach the age of maturity until 1997 so I won't discuss all four tests of faith.

In 1998 as a sophomore at Florida State University (FSU) I learned that I was expecting my first and only child. Earlier in life, due to a medical condition, I was told I would never have a full-term pregnancy. During my first trimester, I was encouraged to terminate my pregnancy after losing twenty-three pounds. I refused. I had two praying grandmothers. I was taught to trust in God. This was my first opportunity to put all my trust in Dr. Jesus. I medically withdraw from FSU, returned to the Jacksonville/Southeast Georgia area, worked part-time to keep my mind right, and attended services regularly with my maternal grandmother. My child was prayed over from November 1998 to February 1999 during weekly church services and nightly revivals. In February 1999, I returned to Tallahassee, Florida where I continued to receive medical treatment. On March 23, 1999, I gave birth to a healthy, happy, and bouncing baby girl. She is currently a college freshman!

In 2010, as an Air Force Reservist following graduate school, I was given a diagnosis of Gastric Cancer (Stage 3 or 4) which changed my life because I had to have a full gastrectomy. On September 15, 2010, my paternal grandmother said to me, "This is your cross, you must carry it."

I had no idea the weight that had been placed upon me. From summer 2009 until September 2010 I was ill, diagnosed with cancer, and I decided to have surgery without telling a single person. As my father, a retired merchant mariner, boarded a flight to be shipped overseas I made the most difficult phone call of my life. His only child had CANCER. Everyone was shocked, concerned, and angry. I tried to fix this alone. I didn't want to burden my loved ones. If my father had not been leaving the country I don't know that I would have disclosed this information before my surgery on October 20, 2010. As instructed, I got my affairs in order, discussed death and dying with my daughter, and kept on my "game face." My surgery was successful. In trying to take care of everything and everyone around me I forgot to take care of me. From a Facebook post in Spring of 2017 just before my daughter's high school graduation: "...Those that had doubt and expressed discouragement JUST look at God. Favor ain't fair! I know my #divainthesky & #mysugarlumpinthesky are beaming with pride just knowing that they raised me to raise my child. I know #myfavoritedeacon is singing his song (our front porch praise); "That's alright, that's alright, since I know I got a seat in God's kingdom, that's alright." I know #myfavoritecarpenter is smiling too. His smile and that Serenity Prayer was all we needed when he would say, "January (that's me) just wait on God." He didn't live to see my cancer journey (10/20/10); he passed away June 12, 2008 only five days after my Nova Southwestern University (NSU-Master of Science in Family Therapy) graduation. I am me because of the house that built me. This solid foundation gave me the reassurance that my baby girl would be just fine even during hospitalization, rehabilitation, and our "new normal." Thank the Lord. Thank her villagers. #JourneyWithJy"

Let the Work That I've Done Speak for Me

According to the Church Covenant I am to contribute to church regularly to support ministry, church expenses, and the relief of the poor. As instructed I began to tithe at a young age and continued to do so until I became disabled in 2012. In addition, I have worked on different ministries within the church; music, dance, and the youth ministry. I also started a grassroots nonprofit organization in 2008 following my graduate school graduation in Jacksonville, Florida; "Connecting the Dots of Jacksonville (CTD)." Although I no longer tithe, I do contribute regularly through CTD to worthy causes. The CTD mission is connect people, places, and things in the areas of community improvement, youth initiatives, writer's development/book publishing, organizational management, and grant writing. In addition to my church's music ministry, I was a member of my middle school and high school choruses in predominantly African American schools in Jacksonville, Florida. I performed in other organizations through my undergraduate studies. Music continues to be medicine to my mind, body, and soul.

What A Friend We Have In Jesus

During the course of my medical journey I learned to self-soothe since I kept a whole lot to myself for the first year. After my diagnosis my coping mechanisms included spending a lot of time at the beach or near a lake, walking, listening to music, and self-reflection. After the isolation started to get the best of me I needed another avenue in which I could express my brewing frustrations without having to actually talk to another person. Journaling became a very valuable tool for me. I would just write for hours as I thought about what happened and what was to come. The more I wrote the better I started to feel. The only friend I had at this time was Jesus. I have often heard others say that they have heard directly from Jesus. I can't attest to that. An example of Jesus's presence came most recently as I was recovering from my latest medical episode. My last grandparent, my maternal grandmother, passed away in November 2016. I thought of her most recently in February since she would have celebrated her 90th birthday this year. I rarely rest well during medical episodes. I had a dream about my grandmother, after a drastic Celiac flare up this year (2018) I could not walk for a significant amount of time. During this dream we talked and sang one of her favorite hymns. I could feel her presence even after waking up. I attribute these types of refreshing and reassuring moments to Jesus. The same way my grandmother covered me on earth she is now covering me in the afterlife. During significant medical episodes such as this one which included hospitalization, rehabilitation, and followed by home health, I found myself very discouraged. No inspirational song reached me. I was not by bubbly self. I was sleep deprived, frustrated, and in despair. I continued to go through the motions of daily life because quitting has never been an option for me. I mean never. Doctors have given up on me. Family has given up on me. Friends have given up on me. My motivation (Jyra) has been looking back at me for the past 18 years and she will continue to look to me even as an adult. Jyra is the air that I breathe and the reason I keep that friend in Jesus.

Trouble In My Way I Have To Cry

Sometimes Folks say, "Jan you post (on Facebook) some sincere sounding prayers," and I reply, "Turn your Bible to Proverbs, Chapter 22 and read verse 6; According to scripture if I was trained as a child I would continue as an adult." Any more questions? I DO NOT play with religion every Sunday like a lot of people but my church (my heart) is solid and my faith (hope for peace on earth and salvation in the afterlife) endures. When you can look back over your life and can honestly say your good days outweigh your bad days; your offspring has been properly trained and aren't running amuck; can look at your loved ones and know your contributions made them smile; you know that you have loved your friends; you know that you have even loved your enemies; your belief system gave you hope rather than hate; you made it through your valley experience(s); received your restoration; as you reflect over your journey you can thank God for your deposits and thank God even more for your withdrawals. You have accomplished something to be proud of; YOU SURVIVED! Take the time out to take inventory. Don't block your blessings looking behind you (past) or ahead of you (future) rather get you some right now (present) praise! "He's" been good to me right now! Embracing religion is a good thing. You don't have to overdo it. "His" mercy has kept us all. The oxygen supply is universal and we all put on pants one leg at time. Lean not on your own understanding while letting "Him" direct your path; don't move so fast you leave "Him" behind.

As for me and my house we don't participate in organized religion as much now as we did when Jyra was younger. I don't agree with double-talking undereducated preachers who say they are "called." I believe that authentic pastoring requires a man/woman to be chosen by God. If my lightbulb goes off I politely remove myself from the congregation. Where you go will determine how you grow. In my intimate relationships, although we may not seem Godly we are God-centered and that's what matters most. Embracing a religion and being religious ain't the same thing. There's a difference between personal worship and fellowshipping. The latter requires more than one person.

Keeping that into perspective, I've never claimed to be saved, sanctified, or filled with the Holy Ghost. First off, I'm simply me. Secondly, I've never had a bible thumping male significant other, role model before my maternal grandfather became a Baptist deacon, or absolutely Godly friends. And lastly, since my #cancersurvivor journey I do not attend church services regularly when I feel bad. I will say I was afforded a religious foundation. I know all the United Methodist Church (UMC) and Missionary Baptist Church (MBC) rituals and order of services. I was also regularly exposed to African Methodist Episcopal (AME). If it were not for the Lord on my side since 2008 I don't know where I would be. I'm not perfect, I've made mistakes, I'm spoiled rotten and I believe that the world revolves around me and Jyra. My father calls me daily to remind me I do not need nobody but God, him, family, and friends like family. I acknowledge some of my "play family" before I acknowledge my "blood family" because I was taught to love those who loves me. I have raised an independent, spoiled, and wise-beyond-her-years daughter who will tell you off with a smile, while staying in a child's place. Through it all we have faith that things will always work out for our good.

I've Come This Far By Faith

In a message delivered to high school graduates, *"Never Graduate From God,"* the messenger said, "Life unfortunately looks totally different from school. It will test you without telling you. It will inspect your faith and beliefs. It will examine your morals and values. Life is not considerate enough to provide you weather days. It will promise you sunshine and rain on your parade. Therefore, in all of your doings make continuously seeking God your priority not an option," Courtesy of Pastor Gary Williams.

This message continues to resonate with me because it is truly the testament to my ability to travel my journey. When I look back over my life I can remember many situations that didn't go quite as I had envisioned them. Turns out I have always had what is needed within me to weather the storms of life. I have dealt with the bad things by embracing the good things every step of the way. This is what I call "mustard seed faith."

Once the hospital chaplain came into my room and asked me how it was that I was able to be so positive and cheerful during such a difficult time. It was during the holiday season in 2013. I had been hospitalized on and off since my Celiac flare up began. I was released from the hospital on Christmas Day 2013 only to find myself back in the hospital on January 2, 2014. I recall my oncology surgeon leaving the room telling me that there was nothing more that he could do for me since he felt he had repeated the same surgeries time and time again to no avail. He did not plan to treat me any further. The chaplain asked me what my plan did I have. I told him that I would keep the faith; I had come this far by faith.

Bread of Heaven: Jehovah Jireh the Lord Will Provide

When I started to having symptoms that came with my cancerous stomach I had an ah-ha moment! A little voice said, "The church is in your heart sugar." I didn't realize it at the time but that was the beginning of my showing the onlookers more of "Him" and less of me. The more I felt bad the less church services I attended. I had a routine of listening to gospel music, reading and dissecting my scriptures, and my little talks with Jesus. In the meantime, folks especially those that assumed my issues were psychological rather than physical started rumors about why, who, or what was keeping me from the church (the building). While "they" (folks at church, family members, and so-called friends) were assuming, I was pressing toward the mark on my terms. As a more mature Christian I realized that I did not need a "support group" to praise God. Well to sum it up, I can now tell you what church services I have attended and where I attended in the last several years. When my name is called on "Judgement Day" I am ready to hear, "Servant well done!" Religion, like most things, is a process. Embrace the process, earn the praise!

Funny thing is folks are always asking me if I named "Jyra" (sounds like Jireh) her name because of my religious beliefs or because my mom's name is Ira. All I know for certain is there has always been the favor of the Lord over Jyra's life. At the end of each and every phone call for the six months of my recovery from October 2010 to April 2011 my granny would say, "The Lord will provide (as long as you keep doing right by your baby, He's going to keep doing right by you)." I listened!

The Bible says to honor your "parents." Common sense tells me to honor my "parents." Just because you participated in creating a child does not mean you "parented" that child. I refer to my biological parents as my chosen vessels and I refer to myself as a "village baby." I was extremely close to both sets of my grandparents since childhood. Remarkably I was blessed to have all four of them until age 29. The tenth anniversary of my grandfather's death is in June. I continue to honor my deceased grandparents and my other villagers as one should honor their parents. My biological father is my rock and I speak to and of him often.

I thank God for the men on my team. Ain't nothing like being covered by God's love thru his love for God. There is a difference between being religious and being spiritual (and churchgoers they are not). As long as I know that "they" know what an awesome God we serve everything will continue to work out for the good! I will remain single, unmarried, and wait on The Lord. If you are attracted to me and you approach me and you "ain't got no religion" just keep going. If you will be a part of my life you must have a supreme being that you serve; meaning bigger than you and I. I learned one of my most valuable religious lessons from one of these men. It is not how you fight the battle but with whom you fight the battle that matters most. Some folks get being spiritual (believing) and religious (churchy) confused...some of these folks are going to miss the mark! Sinners have souls too...we are ALL SAVED BY GRACE!

No Charge

I learned some of my most important life lessons while sitting observing my grandmother as she would cook, sing, and dance in a kitchen at home or work. Cooking was her love language. She accomplished so much more than just preparing a good tasting meal. In our little talks she stressed putting God first, honoring your husband, loving your family, being a productive employee, showing yourself friendly, and so much more. She was my granny and I was her shadow. Like a sponge I absorbed it all. I have inherited an endless supply of wisdom and recipes. I am forever grateful. In later years, once healing became my focus she became more than just someone I listened to but someone who listened to me. She encouraged me to let it all out. To either put it in someone else's ear so that they could help me carry my cross or find something else to do to divert my energy. I had a bar stool for resting, good set of pots for cooking, and box full of her recipes to put the soul in the soul food. With those tools I began to cook. Although I am not always able to eat because of my GI issues like my grandmother I find so much peace in the kitchen. Just to smell, the aroma, and seeing the joy that "good eating" (as my grandmother would call it brings others) brings me so much joy. There was no charge for my grandmother's unconditional love just like there's no charge for God's love.

Healing

Richard Smallwood sings, "No matter what your friends might say don't believe them because God's got a healing for you." I had to believe in my healing when nobody else believed in it far too many times. No matter what it was that was said time and time again I have always believed that even if my body is never fully restored there will always be healing for my soul. Although some can only see the test in each situation I am learning during every valley experience to see the testimony that comes after each situation. God's promise of full restoration has kept me over the last seven years while living without a stomach.

Grief
Demetria Hill Cannady, PhD, LPC

Grief is an intense emotional loss characterized by sorrow and distress. People experience grief from situations other than the death of a loved one. Grief presents itself in everyday situations: job loss, relocation, money issues, ending of relationships (to include friendships), marital affairs, breakups and divorce to name a few. You must be able to identify grief and the stages of grief when it presents so that you can effectively manage your emotions and the emotions associated with grief.

According to Elizabeth Kubler-Ross, there are five stages of grief which Elizabeth Kubler-Ross (On Death and Dying, 1969) discusses which are: denial and isolation; anger; bargaining; depression; and acceptance. **Denial** is a defense mechanism in which a person ignores or disavows unacceptable thoughts or acts as if an experience does not exist or never did. **Isolation** is a style of living in which a person is disconnected socially and emotionally from others; a defense mechanism that people employ to separate an idea from its emotional content. **Anger** occurs in an explosion of emotion, where the bottled-up feelings of the previous stages are expulsed in a huge outpouring of grief. **Bargaining** is parting with something after negotiation but get little or nothing in return. Depression is characterized by sadness, dejection, lack of energy, hopelessness, and loneliness. Depression can be chronic or acute, mild or severe. **Acceptance** is a deep and genuine caring for a client as a person; a simple acknowledgement by the counselor of the clients' previous statement with a "yes" response that encourage the client to continue; acknowledges what is happening in a counseling session as opposed to evaluating it.

There is also a model titled the "Final Stage Model," which was discussed on the website, www.recover-from-grief.com, which no specific author mentioned but information which related to seven stages of grief. These stages include: shock and denial; pain and guilt; anger and bargaining; depression, reflection, and loneliness; the upward turn; reconstruction and working through; and acceptance and hope. There were seven stages of grief as it related to an individual experiencing an affair: shock; denial; bargaining; guilt; anger; depression; and acceptance. Allison Williams shared her seven stages of grief as it relates to individuals going through a divorce: "denial; pain and fear; anger; bargaining; guilt; depression; and acceptance," (www.livestrong.com).

I think whatever reason an individual experiences grief, it can present and manifest as anxiety, anger, come in the form of crying spells, fatigue, lack of energy, guilt, loneliness, pain, sadness, and you may have trouble sleeping. Please do not attempt to go through the grief stages alone; seek the help of supportive family and friends, along with talking to a therapist or your pastor/ spiritual leader. Grief will often return through memories and everyday events, sometimes manifesting in the form of smells, songs, and places. This grief will cause emotions to arise which you thought that you'd conquered. Rest assured that it is therapeutic to talk about the loved one that died or left the relationship. Accept the feelings which you feel and do not feel guilty about your feelings. Continue to take care of yourself and your loved ones by not becoming stagnant and stuck after the passing of the loved one. Reach out to others for help and support; ask for help. Some people want to assist but are waiting to know that they are needed as not to invade your space or overwhelm you in your time of grief. Most importantly, celebrate the life that the person lived instead of focusing on the fact that they are no longer with you.

There will be birthdays, anniversaries, and special dates where our memories of the loved one may cause us to experience grief. These events will occur at least annually so have a plan in place to deal with these challenging times. Prepare yourself mentally and emotionally prior to these dates arriving. Plan a distraction whether is consists of a small informal dinner or a celebration of life event. It is good to reminisce on the good times with your loved one, for the memories will always be with you. Start a new tradition such as a short getaway or vacation during these times which would normally bring you sadness. Most importantly, allow yourself to feel and experience the emotions associated with your grief but do not allow the emotions to totally consume you. Grieve and move forward afterwards.

References:

Kubler-Ross, Elizabeth, 1969. On Death and Dying.

The Five Stage Model, 2017. Retrieved from: https://www.recover-from-grief.com

I was born on the August 28, 1964 in Quitman, Georgia. My parents are Robert Rose and Roberta Hill. I have experienced the greatest thing in life and that is to give birth to four beautiful children in three pregnancies. I am very confident and dedicated individual that love people, love to have fun, make others laugh but more so doing the work of the Lord. Through my pregnancies, I have two sons and two daughters. I am proud grandmother and I love my grands to the utmost; they are my rocks and help to keep me balanced. Although, I had four children, my oldest son which is a twin to my daughter, has gone to heaven at the age of 33 and my remaining children continue to make my life brighter and loving me as a mother and grandmother.

I have attended many schools in my endeavors to gain knowledge that will be beneficial to me and others in the long run. My family believes with all the education that I have I should have my doctoral degree by now. They keep me laughing, however, with knowledge I know that no one can take that from me. I have certifications in Childcare, Accounting, Cosmetology, Medical Assistant. I have a certification as a Director of Voluntary Pre-Kindergarten, as well. I attended Jacksonville Theological Seminary and obtained a degree in ministry. I have a Bachelor's Degree in Psychology and Human Services with the Specialization in Social Work. I recently completed my Master Degree in Education with the Specialization in Family and Community Services as well as teach fulltime in a Kindergarten setting. This is my passion because it allows me to help other with a hand up and not a hand out. I have an undying love for God's people and that I believe that no matter what everyone has a small bit of good in them, but the choice comes up to them to walk and produce it in the will of God.

Through my life's journey, I have worked in many settings, but the most rewarding were my jobs as a teacher and a business owner. I was led by God to open a business that assisted people with disabilities. In my heart, these are the people that are given up on in life and made to feel unloved and unwanted. It is not their fault that God made them special. We all are special in our own way but unfortunately some of them had some mental and physical challenges that ill-informed people do not know how to accept. But I thank God for the passion and compassion that He gave me to be able to go and make these individuals feel wanted and loved. Honestly, that is my reason for becoming a teacher because many of our young babies are in the same boat as the disabled due to the dysfunctional families and young parents that have no clue as how to be parents or care for themselves.

This has also afforded me the opportunity to become a motivational speaker to many young adults especially females that have a feeling of hopelessness, low self-esteem, and low morale about life. God gave me the vision of "I Matter Empowerment" that helps to motivate and empower others in knowing that He is the ultimate key. I share a transparent life of all the things I have encountered from being a young child to an adulthood. Some of the things I have encountered, many would not believe that I have overcome sexual abuse, domestic violence, teen pregnancy, drug addiction, suicidal tendencies, homelessness and incarceration. To see what God has done seems to open doors for them to want more and to desire a life free from the mental illness that plagues them. Mental illness is truly many of the reasons why we do some of the things we do in life because we ultimately allowed the enemy to overpower our thought process with negativity. It takes a sold-out mindset to do a paradigm shift to regain power over the obstacles. I know for a fact if I can do it, so can you. God has no respecter or person, and if He can do it for me, He can do it for the very next person. There is absolutely nothing too hard for God. The key factor in the entire equation is. "Are you ready for the change?" "Are you willing to surrender it all to God for greater and better?"

If you are interested in having me to come out and speak to your group, please feel free to contact me at the following email address: imatterempowerment@gmail.com or feel free to contact me via Facebook: I Matter Empowerment.

Looking forward to hearing from you all and thanks for your purchase of the book that I have had a chance to participate in its creation.

I Don't Look Like What I Have Been Through

Rebecca Rose, MA. Ed

My name is Rebecca Rose, and I was born on the 28th of August 1964 in Quitman, Georgia. I was born a female and proud to be one of the greatest creations ever. I am grateful and humble to be allowed life to exist as God's precious gift; I do not take that for granted. My parents are Robert Rose and Roberta Hill. I am blessed to have both of my parents around. I have experienced many things in this life, but the greatest thing is the birth of my four beautiful children in three pregnancies. My age in calculation with my birth year would be 52, and through these pregnancies, I have two sons and two daughters. I was a teenage mother with a lot of tough times, but I made it with the prayers of my grandmother and others. I had my twins at the age of fifteen, and it was a scary and rocky life. My oldest son, who is a twin to my daughter, has gone to Heaven at the age of 33, and my remaining children have made my life brighter and loving my role as a mother and grandmother.

I have encountered many trials in this young life of mine, and the most tragic was the death of my son. It really took a piece of me because you can never imagine losing a child, but I know that reality and life must happen. So, I am so proud to have spent those thirty-three years with him although the doctors had said he wouldn't live to be five years old. For this reason, I am very grateful and proud to be a mother who loves and nurture her children to have them wanting to live on despite adversities. I believe that my spiritual background and prayers helped me to keep strong in the times of hardship because I believe in the Word of God. I am a proud mother of four children, Antwaun Rose, Alesia Rose, Nakeisha Stroud and Dwayne Stroud, Jr. However, as I mentioned before, my oldest son, Antwaun Rose is deceased, and this was another thing that turned my world upside down. I am also a proud grandmother of five biological grandchildren,

Ariyannah, Da'Marion, Khaleisha, Khaleik, and Ja'Niyah, plus numerous adopted grands that I love to the moon and back, Shania and Jeremiah.

As a child growing up in rural Georgia, I attended a segregated school and then was bussed to public school. My memory of that was quite frightening because Blacks were treated so unfair during those times, and I had to fight to get my education fairly. While attending the public schools, I had teachers that inspired me because they took the time to show they cared. They impacted me through many aspects but reading the book *The Magic of Thinking Big*, was the topic that really changed my life forever. It inspired me to reach for whatever I desired in life regardless of the obstacles. If I believed it, I could achieve it.

My mom raised all five of her children the best she could with the help of my grandparents who are deceased now, Herbert and Eliza Hill. Her perseverance helped me to be the woman that I am now, yet my grandparents were my rock as well and helped me to believe in myself when no one else did. My early childhood was kind of a hard one for me because my parents split when I was almost eight years old. They (meaning the people of society) say that a child should not remember things that happened so far in the past, but I do remember them, oh so well. That was the turning point in my life because my world had been turned upside down. My mom strenuously worked to make sure that we had what we needed as far as necessities in life, but I felt like I was not a part of the family. Do not get me wrong; I loved my mother with all my heart and would jump through hoops to try to make her proud of me while I was growing up. My childhood was not what I considered normal in my eyesight, but it was what I had grown to know at that present time. I was a child seeking so much attention from whoever would give it to me.

I felt like an outsider for years, but it was only the plot of the enemy to sabotage my life to have me go spiraling uncontrollable through life. My parents' separation made me feel as though it was my fault for many years because back then, it was a taboo for a woman to be unwed and pregnant, so I felt like my parents got married all because of me. I didn't know any better, but to allow the devil to play with my mind. I struggled to make them both love me or take notice but everything failed in my eyesight. I hated myself, and I hated the world that I was living in because my mind was fixated that no one loved me, and no one cared whether I lived or died. This story about my life may not sit well with some, but I must tell it to help someone overcome the obstacles of low self-esteem, low self-respect, and no love for living.

I love my family, but I allowed the enemy to throw darkness on my life because I found out that I was named after a biblical woman, and my name had power. The enemy attacks those that are called by God and have divine purpose on Earth. I believe my calling is to help to bring peace to families where the enemy has infiltrated and cause much havoc. My vision is to help to inspire, empower and educate youth and young adults with healthy behaviors, life skills, and tools that will aid in their development and self-esteem, so they can bloom to their full potential.

I am a motivator of many because I love helping families achieve goals by providing a strong support system. My Master's Degree is just one thing I will have achieved because I promised myself and my son that is deceased that I would conquer it. I know with this degree, it will open many more doors of opportunity for me to help others and gain knowledgeable resources to help families within the school and the community. I am currently a Kindergarten teacher in Florida, and I love making a difference in the lives of the young. I chose to teach because this is a field whose training will help me help others, especially our youth. Many of our youth are being raised by parents that are babies themselves and lack skills to be parents so that causes children to lack the necessities needed to be successful and that is mainly "LOVE. I believe children should know love and feel loved at an early age so that their lives and education can matter most to them.

There are so many children that are suffering because they feel that they are not loved, and they lack confidence to make the right choices in life. This is something I can identify with very well because unlike them, my mother and father loved me, but I built a wall to not receive the love.

I look back over my life, and I feel that I missed out on so much. My mom and I did not have a relationship back then all because of this wall the enemy placed between us. I must say that forgiveness has given me the opportunity to get a relationship started with her, and I am loving every minute of it. I never hated her, but I just felt rejected by her because when my parents split, damaging words were said by both, and they damaged me and my self-esteem. I vowed to never allow a child to feel what I felt growing up, and I intend to keep that promise to God and myself.

I am currently known as "MOMMA ROSE" to many because of my loving and nurturing nature. I love being me and what God has called me to be. I do have some fond memories of growing up because I had grandparents that loved me unconditionally. My grandmother was my inspiration, and she showed me what a real wife and mother should exemplify. I was a teenaged mother of twins, and it was quite difficult, but my grandparents took me in and helped me to achieve my goal of getting my high school diploma. Many people had counted me out when I got pregnant, but my grandparents made sure that I got my education and paid for me to attend trade school afterwards.

Turning Point of My Life

I can remember my grandmother taking me to church with her back in the country, St. Phillips A.M.E. church. That was my first encounter with God and trying to find ways to please the people who mattered most in my life. I remember getting her hymnal, and the first song I learned was "Lord, I want to Be a Christian." (A Negro Slave Songs in the United States (1953),

Miles Mark Fisher suggests that this African American spiritual could well have originated in Virginia in the 1750s, based on this story from Hanover, Virginia, 1756: "A black slave asked Presbyterian preacher William Davies). This song was my first encounter of wanting to live right and be like Jesus. I would sing this song continuously as I went through life situations. I felt a calling on me then but did not understand how to make it come to the forefront. My grandmother always told me that I was blessed, and God will always see me through whatever I went through. But who would have known all that I would encounter on this journey called life? I have been through teen pregnancy, three marriages, sexual abuse, domestic violence, suicide attempts, drug abuse, homelessness, and the loss of my grandparents and my child.

At the age of fifteen years old, a guy came along that saw my vulnerability and played on it. Here I am a fat, low self-esteemed young girl looking for someone to love me, and I fell for him. I became pregnant and that caused a new level of hurt and bitterness in my life. I have now disappointed my mother and disgraced the family, but no matter what, I was going to keep my children. I was called everything but a child of God after my pregnancy came to light. I tried to hide it from my mother and the people around me, but you know what they say, "What's done in the dark will come to life," and it did at seven months. I gave birth to twins, a boy and a girl. I had an encounter with God because I was losing my daughter. The doctors said that she may not make it through the night. I would fast and pray, not even knowing what that meant. I did it because I stayed in the Word of God, and I believed His Word. The Bible told me that Peter kneeled in Acts 9:40 and prayed, and the damsel was awakened. Then Jesus, in Matthew 9:25 spoke to the deceased child, and she got up. I relied on Matthew 6:6, that states "But when you pray, go into your inner room, shut your door, and pray to your Father, who is unseen. And your Father, who sees what is done in secret, will reward you," (NIV). I believed God and took Him literally at His word. I prayed and prayed, and God delivered my daughter.

As soon as she was out the woods, I was hit with the news about my son which was that he was diagnosed with cerebral palsy. I began to blame myself because I was so ruthless and defiant to my mother because the Bible tells us in Ephesian 6:1-3 to "1-Children, obey your parents in the Lord: for this is right; 2-Honour thy father and mother; (which is the first commandment with promise); 3-That it may be well with thee, and thou mayest live long on the earth, (NIV). I was, in my eyesight, being punished for my rebellious nature, for defying what my mother had tried to tell me. Here I am a single mother of two, both with medical issues, but I vowed to love them and be there for them regardless of what happens in my life. My son began to have seizures and the doctors told me that I needed to put him in a facility where he would cared for because I was too young, but the devil was and still is a liar. I said, "No, if I was big enough to lay there and get them, I am big enough to take care of them." I refused to give my babies away. All the solutions they were giving made sense, but I am not like most. I felt God gave me my babies to love. I finally had someone to love me in spite of me, and no one would take them away from me. I had begun to become bitter and broken because I knew that I loved God, and that God had me, but why did He allow me to go through so much. My first attempt of suicide happened when I was in eighth grade. I hated that I had no one I could turn too. All my "so-called friends" had parents that they could go and talk to, but I felt all alone, unloved and unwanted. My question then was why should I live? I did attempt, and the attempt was stopped by my Godmother who saw my hurt and reached out to me.

After all this, five years later, I became pregnant and gave birth to my beautiful daughter. I did not want to paint a picture of the unwed young girl with a house full of children. I was already told that I would not amount to anything, I would not finish high school, and I would have a house full of children by the age of 25. I finished high school, vocational school, and yes, I had four children by the time I was 23. I attended a technical school and studied accounting because I thought I wanted to do that but found out all that math was no joke. I graduated because my grandfather said he didn't raise a quitter, and quitting was not an option. I later married the father of my daughter; my mother did not like him, but out of spite, I married him. He was mentally abusive, and then it became physical, but I stayed because I did not want to be like my mother— divorced with children to raise on my own. I had begun to hate that I was born. My husband introduced me to drugs: marijuana, and then crack cocaine.

I was so out of touch with everything. The enemy had me going in circles because I left God because all this was too much to handle. Yes, I said I left God, but He was there all the time carrying me and holding me when I didn't think He was anywhere near. When I became pregnant with my son, and his namesake, President Carter was putting people, especially women who had a child born with drugs in their system, in prison, I fell to my knees, prayed and sought the face of Jesus because that was not the life I wanted, and I wanted better for me and my children. I didn't have to go to rehab although there's nothing wrong with rehab, but I chose Jesus. Hallelujah!!!! I cried out to him like the woman with the issue of blood that had suffered for twelve long years (Matthew 9:20). I reached out to touch His garment so that I could be made whole. I didn't want to be subject to that lifestyle again.

My husband then didn't have a partner anymore because the scales fell off my eyes, and I could see clearly. I wanted to live, and I wanted to have a drug-free life and freedom. My husband became abusive then and would threaten to kill me. I overlooked it because it was a threat towards me and not the children. One day, it became detrimental; I came home from work, and he wanted my paycheck, but I refused to give it to him. He backslapped me across the table, and I was pregnant with his child at that time. I got up and took a stand. Somehow, I got to a plate and threw it, and it broke, but he was cut, and I didn't know how it happened. I knew then it was time for change. I stayed a few more days, then one night, he came in and threatened to burn me and my children up in the house. As long as the threats were against me, I was fine, but it took another turn, and God made a way of escape for me. I left there and never returned. I was free from him and free from drugs.

Even after all God had done for me, I yet ran. I began going to the clubs and hanging out with friends. I had freedom, but I was not free. I had pimped God to get me out of something, and that is what some of us do today. We use God as if He's a slot machine or a genie we can spin or rub and get what we want. I am so guilty of this behavior. I then became an alcoholic and smoked marijuana. I was a wretch undone and really trying to medicate my pain with drugs and alcohol because of the pain I was experiencing deep within. The party life became old and by the age of 28, I was done with that lifestyle and totally free from drugs and alcohol. I wanted better for me and my children. I wanted to be somebody and make my children proud to call me momma.

Unfortunately, I kept ending up with guys that didn't mean me any good. I went from one type of abuse to the next. Looking for love in all the wrong places. I began to go through stages of depression that caused me to shut down and not want to live. I made more bad choices in my life where I had to spend time away from my children, and I went to jail. Yes, I said it; I went to jail for stupidity, and I survived. God has a way to bring us back to Him and to help us to get our lives together. Even though I was working to get my sanity back, the enemy was constantly telling me that I was worthless and taunt me as to why I was still alive. The next attempt came when I was grown and on my own. I took the medication, Theo-dur, which is an asthma medication. I took a total of 6 pills. By the time I called my cousin, a woman of God, to whom I called to say good bye, she knew that something was wrong. She got me to the ER, and the doctors said that two pills should have killed me, but I survived. All of this was a cry for help because I hated me, and I was in an abusive relationship. I bounced from one unhealthy relationship to the next. I got married, left him and then got in another unhealthy relationship because I did not want to be alone. It's okay to be alone, friends; that is when God can use you more. I had to come to that realization because the enemy had me mentally on lockdown.

In 1990, the Lord took my grandfather home, and I literally lost my mind. Growing up, he told me that he would never leave me, and I felt that he lied to me. I was in an abusive relationship then, and this person tried to keep me away from my family. Yet, God fixed it. Yes, I got locked up again, and my grandfather's health became worse while I was locked down. I cried out to God to allow me to see my grandfather before He took him home with Him, and He honored that. That is why I know that God hears a sinner's prayer because I was full of sin. I repented and turned my face to the wall once more, and He gave me my heart's desire and that was to see my grandfather alive. I got out of jail, and the guy I was in a relationship with broke my jaw, and my face was all distorted. I walked in to see my grandfather at home, and he took one look at me on his death bed and made me laugh. Anyone who knew my grandfather knew he would keep you laughing regardless of his mood. He looked at my face and said, "That ____?! Better be glad I can't get up from here because I would put my big black foot in his ____!" (Fill in the blanks). He made me smile because I knew my grandfather loved me and would always protect me. The day he died, a piece of me died. I lost my mind and had to be put in a facility in Florida for a nervous breakdown. I didn't want to accept the fact that the one man that said he wouldn't leave me, left me. Here I am again, feeling rejected and abandoned. Why is God so mad with me to take people I love away from me and leave me all alone? First, in my mind, He caused my parents to separate, then I got pregnant with sickly children. I got hooked on drugs and married an abusive man followed by other abusive relationships thereafter. Why God hated me was how I related my life to what was happening. I can say then I literally hated God for taking my grandfather, but I am so glad that He knew my heart. I was a lost soul. I didn't want to live anymore because no one could or would love me like my granddaddy. Not realizing that God loved me all the time, and He was carrying me through it all with my disobedient self.

After I left the facility, I ran away from home. Literally, I moved and didn't let anyone know where I was going but my uncles. They helped me pack and hid my children and me until I left the state of Georgia. I had no clue where I was going, but I prayed to God to lead me if I was to survive. I was led to a small town in Florida called Crystal River where God had angels waiting to take my small family in and love us. It is here where God became my all, and I didn't look back. I found my relationship with God, and I loved how it made me feel. I had started loving me somewhat, but my relationship with God was beautiful. Although, I went with little to no money in my pocket, God sustained me and my babies. I knew it was Him that sent me there, and I gained back some self-dignity and love for myself. I met families that helped to spiritually mold me into the woman of God that I am now. While there, I enrolled in the childcare classes and completed it, but grew weary because trying to raise children and take care of a terminally ill son was too much, so I briefly stopped until his health got better. I then pursued a career in Cosmetology, and I loved it, but it became old and boring to me. Later, I decided that I would go to school to get my degree in special education and that seem to be where I really loved to be. I attended college and received my AA in Liberal Arts and AS in Social Work then the inevitable happened my son became ill again and almost died, so I quit school once more. I moved from Crystal River, Florida to Leesburg, Florida where God had even more in store for me. I began to get my self-confidence back. God placed me in a church to gain knowledge of ministry and how ministry was to be conducted. I left that ministry because the teachings were not what God had placed in my spirit because I truly felt my relationship with Him. After thinking I left in good faith, the enemy spread lies to the new ministry which I became part of, but I thank God for an overseer that had a relationship with God. My Bible told me, "And I will give you pastors according to mine heart, which shall feed you with knowledge and understanding," (Jeremiah 3:15 NIV). I sought God wholeheartedly before I transitioned ministries. This is something that we all need to do in all our dealings in life. When we keep God first and at the forefront, the things we encounter will not overwhelm us. My pastor now was feeding me the unadulterated word of God, and I loved ministry even more.

Unfortunately, my stay in Leesburg was short-lived, and we moved to Gainesville, Florida. My son's life had begun to go "topsy turvy", and I was spending more times at Shands Hospital; I was away from work more than anything else. After his health stabilized, I was able to go back to school, and I finished my Bachelor Degree in Human Services with a Specialization in Social Work and my minor in Psychology. I guess that was my calling to help others and to make sure that people get a fair shake in life. I love working with people and seeing them gain self-worth and a new passion for life. My passions in life are my family, especially my grandchildren, helping children hold on to their dreams and never giving up, and inspiring young people to reach for the stars. I have a passion to work with young females to let them know that their lives matter. I believe if I would have placed my son in a facility, he would not have lived past the age of five, but God gave him longevity because he knew love, and it was my appointed destiny to make sure he knew love.

However, the day that God decided to take my son, I felt my world was over. I knew he was suffering, but he had survived so many times before. They put him in hospice so many times before, and he survived years afterwards, so this time was no different. I went to see him at my friend's house because she was helping me to care for him while I recovered from surgery. I knew that he would bounce back. My son had gone through multiple comas due to medications, and he experienced many seizures due to lack of medications. In my opinion, he was a guinea pig for medical research, but regardless, he still was surviving. The memory of his death is like a recorder which plays in my head. My son died two days after my shoulder surgery, and I was not able to hold him one last time. His brother drove me to see him and spend time with him that day. I hate I didn't get to hold my child one last time. I didn't know that my last time holding him would be the day before my surgery. We planned to have his 34th birthday party in three days because I knew he would still be here. The call I received, "to come quick because he was unresponsive," sent a piercing knife through my heart. As I walked in, I could feel a different atmosphere in the house. I went to my son and called his name, but he didn't respond; the EMT's were there and there was nothing that could be done. I screamed and got angry with God. What hit me more was the fact that his twin sister who was in living in Atlanta called me right at 2:30 p.m., and the only words she could mutter was, "Mom, my brother." She knew a part of her was gone. During the transitioning, God prepared her and me, but I was not willing to accept the fact that my son was gone. Even through this, the enemy tried his best to take my mind. From what I was told, reality had left me briefly. I say for about two months, I fought with the fact my son is gone. Then, one day while sitting in church, the Spirit of the Lord whispered in my ear, right after I asked God why did He take my son before his 34th birthday, and the small still voice said to me, "My son was 33 when I took Him, and He, just like your son I loaned you, knew no sin." That was the true turning point in my life forever. As of that day, I stopped feeling sorry for myself. I stopped feeling like I didn't matter. I stopped allowing people to dictate what they thought I should do or be. I stopped allowing myself to feel inadequate because of my weight; so what if I am not a size 8. I am still wonderfully and beautifully made in the eyesight of God. God's word lets me know this in Psalms 139:14, "I praise you because I am fearfully and wonderfully made; your works are wonderful, I know that full well," (NIV).

Through my son's death, I began to live because in a dream I had following his death, he spoke to me. Some may say that it is weird because that doesn't happen. But I know it happened, and there was a purpose behind it. My son stated to me to live. My son has never talked or walked, but in this dream, he did both. I thought I had been living, but I guess I wasn't. My entire life had been centered on making others happy and loving everyone else, but I had forgotten to love me. I thought I was living, but I was only existing. Life as I knew it died. I just wanted to make my son proud of me by doing what he had asked me in my dream. We must stop just existing and begin to live. God wants us to be real in all we do for Him and His people. He already knows what we are going to do before we even do it, but one thing I have learned in all this is that a relationship with God is priceless.

My son's death brought unity between my family and me. I had to forgive them and then forgive myself although they may not know what they did to cause me pain. I had to get that forgiveness for me. I started living and living starts with forgiveness. Today I can go home to Georgia and spend quality time with my family. I believe the life that I grew up with helped me to want to show and give love to others. Growing up in my family, I always felt like an outsider because there was a lot of friction between my mom and me after she and my father separated. I decided that I would help others to see their self-worth no matter what others think or believe. It all starts with believing in yourself and moving forward.

My mother did her best to raise her five children without my father. My grandmother raised nine children along with my grandfather, and she was the true matriarch of the family. She strived to keep the family together and loving each other. My mother was a single mother and sacrificed a lot for my siblings. My sister and I are very strong and independent women; she and I raised our children as single parents. I come from a strong biblical background because we reverence God in all things, and I feel that without the prayers and the beliefs of my ancestors, I would not have the strong will to be an example for many. My favorite saying is, "A family that prays together, stays together," (Peyton). I am a firm believer to that being true. I am so thankful for the opportunity to have such a loving family. But it took God to allow me to see where I came from and where I am going. Although I allowed the enemy to reign in my heart and mind for many years with hatred towards my family, I thank God for deliverance and forgiveness.

What is forgiveness? According to Webster, forgiveness is allowing room for error or weakness. I was weak and allowed thoughts that were impure to infiltrate my thought process causing a rift in the life that God had given me. The Bible tells us we should forgive, but how can we when people do us wrong and repeatedly taunt us making us feel like we really don't matter? It is time that we take a stand and realize that God is the only key. Is it easy? No, not by far because people and life will push you to the limits of wanting to end it all. I am a witness to all of it. I have given so much of myself to people only to feel unloved, unwanted, and unappreciated. When I thought life was over, it seemed as though God gave me a fresh wind. I cried out to Him just like David until my eyes were swollen, and my head hurt. I laid there until He gave me a refreshing. I knew that God was there, but sometimes it felt like He was so far from me and that He left me to defend for myself. We must come to know that it is then He is carrying us through the storm. I have wanted to just drop off the end of the earth because of the heartache caused by family and failed relationships. When I sit back and think about things, God does not want me to dwell on what was but to focus on what is to come.

When I came into the real relationship with God, I was able to see much clearer and gain strength from every step I take. So what they left me? I am still not alone. So what I got bills I can't pay? Well, what's for me is for me. So what my children are acting like pure monkeys? God has them because I have given them to Him. Yes, I will continue to uplift them in prayer. When it comes to the decisions they make, the outcome is what they chose when not walking in the will of God. We as parents will always want the best for our children, but I had to learn that we must let them go and let them follow their own paths. We want to forewarn them and keep them from the pain we have encountered, but it's not our lives. I held on trying to keep my children safe and their lives free from trouble so much so that it caused me to have serious health issues. I looked older because of the stress. When I surrendered my life totally to God, I felt the freedom in letting go. I had always heard the cliché, "Let go; Let God" but never fully understood it until I did it. Today, my stress levels have decreased. I am truly free in my spirit. That is what God truly wants from us, to allow Him to reign completely in our lives. He wants to be the one that answers the tough questions of "Why?" when situations hit our lives.

We must just surrender our will to God so that He can lead us in all truth. We can overcome any obstacle if we allow God to lead us. I am so thankful that the times I wanted to end my life, God said "No." I am so thankful for each trial that I encountered because it was then He was making me to be the woman of God that He ordained from my birth. The enemy was upset because I had this calling on my life and that like Job, he could not touch my soul because my heart belongs to God. My loyalty belongs to God. He keeps on blessing me even when I do not see it. Every day that I awaken, I am blessed. Each time I take a breath, I have overcome something that was supposed to take me out.

Although, I went through all the trials, there were many more that I encountered that was supposed to end my life, but God's grace and His mercy kept me. My words to you, my friend, is do not allow the challenges that life throws at you, determine your outcome. Set your mind and heart on God. Allow Him to literally fight your battles for you and while in the fire, continue to praise Him. When the words can't come from your mouth, speak it in your mind. Honestly, that is one place that the enemy cannot read. When we speak it in the atmosphere, there are imps assigned to our lives to throw blockers up. We must remember we do not fight against flesh and blood.

The Bible informs of this in Ephesian 6:12, "For our struggle is not against flesh and blood, but against the rulers, against the authorities, against the powers of this world's darkness, and against the spiritual forces of evil in the heavenly realms," (NIV). God is the only key to our struggles and to the power to overcome. God is the only one that can make our paths straight when we falter. I encourage you to stay focused and do not allow the mere thoughts of the enemy to cause you to lose hope in God. Hope in God allows us to know that despite the struggle, if we keep our eyes focused on coming through and not sitting still, we will make it through all ordeals in life. I am a witness, and I will continue to move forward and praise Him in all things. He is my source of strength when I am weak. He is my friend when everyone walks out or turns their backs on me. He loves you with an unconditional love. Only man have conditions of how he will love us and how long he will love us. But my God has infinite love and loves me despite my shortcomings and hang ups.

My challenge to you is to try to stay focused and truly sell out to God and allow Him to lead you and be there for you no matter what the challenge may be. You can win at whatever you set your mind to, but it takes a well-made up mind as well as praising God in all things. It is not an easy journey, but if I can do it being a rebellious, stouthearted, hardheaded and bitter woman who overcame the struggle of low self-esteem, abusive relationships, dysfunctional family issues, rape, drug abuse, and party life, YOU CAN DO IT TOO!!!!

I believe in you, so BELIEVE in yourself!

References

Retrieved from: http://hymnary.org/hymn/PsH/264. Psalter Hymnal Handbook. 1987

Retrieved from: http://biblehub.com. Holy Bible, New International Version®, NIV® Copyright © 1973, 1978, 1984, 2011 by Biblica, Inc.

Substance Abuse

Demetria Hill Cannady, PhD, LPC

I've been interested in addictions as far back as my freshman year of college after completing a practicum at the local day program for substance abuse. I would sit in the groups as a co-facilitator while actively listening to the group participants share their journeys of how they became addicted to drugs and their struggles with recovery. From that day forward, all other internships consisted of working with individuals with addictions. Not to mention, there were several individuals on the maternal and paternal sides of my family with substance abuse issues, alcohol and drugs. The Counseling Dictionary defines Substance Abuse as the habitual and often addictive use of alcohol, drugs, and tobacco. Drugs are any substance other than food that can affect the way a person's mind and body works (Gladding, 2006, 137). Drugs include stimulants, depressants, and hallucinogens. Substance abuse issues with women appear to have more complex issues because they have primary (physical or sexual abuse) and secondary (stresses related to work, marriage, children, and responsibilities) layers prior to and in addition to the substance abuse.

Women use alcohol and drugs to self-medicate because of the trauma which they were exposed to or because they experienced trauma as a child, teenager, or in early adulthood. As a child and a teenager, the trauma experienced could be molestation, physical abuse, sexual abuse, witnessing domestic violence, and or loss of a parent to name a few. As an adult, physical abuse, sexual abuse, domestic violence, loss of a child/ spouse/or parent, and divorce to name a few. Individuals can have a genetic predisposition (family history) which increases the likelihood of developing a substance abuse disorder. Women who have substance abuse issues are more likely to have/trigger other mental health issues such as Depression, Anxiety Disorder, Panic attacks, Eating Disorders, and Post Traumatic Stress Disorder (PTSD).

There are a few more gender differences with women who abuse alcohol and drugs versus men with alcohol and drug issues. Susan Ramsey noted, "Women with poor self-esteem is a major issue and contributes to alcohol and drug problems. In addition to, they have a history of physical abuse and sexual abuse. They abuse alcohol following depression, to relax on dates, to feel more adequate, to lose weight, to decrease stress or to help them sleep at the night. Alcohol consumption is most common among women in their 20's and 30's; women who are separated or divorced; women who are unmarried and living with a partner; and women who never married. Women are more vulnerable to alcohol-related brain damage; more likely to develop alcohol-induced liver disease; more likely to develop alcoholic hepatitis and die of cirrhosis of the liver. Women develop heart disease at the same rate with less alcohol consumption than men. Women also have an increased risk of breast cancer which is linked to moderate and heavy alcohol consumption. Women are apt to have babies that or alcohol or drug addicted and must go through withdrawals as they detox from the alcohol or drugs. The babies have the possibilities of being born prematurely; early and/or underweight; can be born with Fetal Alcohol Syndrome (FAS); brain damage, and physical abnormalities," (www.healthywomen.org/condition/substanceabuse).

High school girls are at a higher risk for dating violence when they drink alcohol and/or use drugs. College women (ages 18-25 years old) will binge drink consuming four or more drinks in one two-hour setting or less and they are more likely to be victims of sexual assault/abuse. College students can have death occur because of alcohol poisoning. According to research, responsible drinkers will drink no more than one drink (14 grams, 0.6 fluid ounces, or 1.2 tablespoons = one (1) 12-ounce bottle of beer or wine cooler; 8 to 9 ounces of malt liquor; 5 ounces in a glass of wine; or 1.5 ounces of 80-proof liquor). Women ages 60 years and older suffer with problems with cigarettes, alcohol, and psychoactive prescription drugs (sedatives and tranquilizers). The tranquilizers which are frequently misused or abused are Valium, Librium, and Xanax. Women are more likely to use narcotic pain relievers for non-medical use than men. Older women levels for alcohol consumption decreases with age. (www.healthywomen.org/condition/substanceabuse).

Women have an increased risk for sexually transmitted diseases when they use illicit drugs such as marijuana, cocaine, heroin, as well as, the newer drugs molly and flakka. Also, women tend to misuse and abuse prescription drugs and will mix alcohol and prescription drugs. Women are more likely to overdose than men. More than four (4) million women need treatment for drug problems and the key to their treatment is treating depression and Anxiety Disorder. However, most are reluctant to go to recovery for the fear of losing their children or the fact that they will not be able to care for their children (www.healthywomen.org/condition/substanceabuse).

All the information which has been included within the past few pages are very much true based upon my interactions with women who resided within a long-term residential treatment setting. During my tenure as a Program Manager for a residential treatment facility for women there were numerous women which entered the facility from all walks of life, socioeconomic status, and women of all ages, with the oldest participant being in her sixties. When making inquiries as to how they began using alcohol and drugs, most shared of traumatic experiences which occurred to them in childhood and as teenagers. Some of these stories were so horrific that you felt their pain and often cried with them. There were some who had triggers just by looking at certain types of bottles while others replaced their drug of choice with cigarettes or candy. Some women came with an open-mind wanting treatment while others came to avoid jail time. One individual that I remember was held in jail until a bed space was open for her at the facility; a condition of her probation/release. Ninety-five percent of these women had children, and some had their children with them at the facility. Not only were these women trying to stay clean and sober, but they were trying to parent their children with little to no parenting skills and parent while being alcohol and drug-free- all of which were new experiences.

Most of these women had given up hope and faith in God. In their minds, why would God allow something so traumatic to happen to them if HE is supposed to be a God of love? Some were unforgiving of themselves and the perpetrator. They felt that they deserved what happened to them, "It was my fault." They were children on whom adult men preyed, and no one helped yet accused them of "being fast," or "wanting it!" They were not able to share with anyone what happened due to being threatened about what would happen if they told. Most suffered in silence and continue to suffer in silence because of the fear and shame associated with what happened to them. Some of the ladies started to attend church while in treatment and re-established a relationship with their "Higher Power." Others participated in programs such as *Celebrate Recovery* which is normally held in a church setting and addresses any form of addiction; a Christ-Centered Recovery Program. *Celebrate Recovery* is a ministry of fellowship, teaching, and celebration of healing for life's hurts, habits, and hang-ups. It focuses on recovery within areas of your life focusing on more than alcohol and drugs (www.celebraterecovery.com). If you, as a spiritual leader/minister/pastor, are interested in assisting individuals with addictions in recovery phase, maybe a Celebrate Recovery program can begin within in your ministry.

References:

Gladding, S. 2006. Drugs. *The Counseling Dictionary*, p. 137.

National Women's Health Resource Center (medically reviewed by Ramsey, S.E.), 2017. Substance Abuse. Retrieved from: https://www.healthywomen.org/conditions/substanceabuse

Celebrate Recovery, 2015. Retrieved from: https://www.celebraterecovery.

Kelisa V. Brown is a native of Lakeland, Georgia whom has lived in Valdosta, Georgia for much of her life. Kelisa worked for an educational nonprofit for ten years. It was during this time that she realized that she had a passion for helping at-risk youth fulfill their true potential. Her work experience in the mental health field and as a social services case manager greatly influenced Kelisa to start a non-profit organization, Vision of Hope Mentoring, Inc, to help at-risk youth obtain their GED and assist them with becoming productive citizens in the community. Vision of Hope Mentoring, Inc assists these individuals by ensuring that any unmet mental health needs are addressed, mentoring them, and teaches them academic and job readiness skills.

Kelisa received her Bachelor Degree in General Studies with an emphasis in Psychology, Women's Studies, and Adult Education from Valdosta State University, Valdosta, Georgia. She also earned a Master Degree in Public Administration and Human Resource Management from Keller Graduate School of Management, Downers Grove, Illinois. Kelisa is also currently working towards completing a Doctoral Degree in Public Administration through North Central University, Scottsdale, Arizona.

Kelisa V. Brown is a single parent of four children and three grandchildren. In her spare time, Kelisa enjoys participating in community service organizations such as National Council of Negro Women in which she serves as the local chapter Historian and the Hahira Lowndes County Community Development Outreach Corporation (local Debutante Cotillion) on which she serves as the local chapter Secretary and as the Co-chair of the Fundraiser Department. Kelisa also enjoys serving as the Youth Director of the youth ministry at Lighthouse Christian Fellowship Center. Kelisa is very family oriented and spends a lot of quality time with her family. Kelisa V. Brown can be contacted via email, kvbrown1970@gmail.com.

Vision of Hope

Kelisa Brown, MPA, MHRM

My spiritual journey has not been an easy one. I was first introduced to Christ when I was a very young girl at age four years old. At that stage in my life, I did not know that I was on what would become my spiritual journey in life. As a matter of fact, I did not know what a journey was or what it really meant to be spiritual. I came from a family filled with Pastors, Ministers, Evangelists, Elders, Missionaries, Prophets, and Prayer Warriors. Although my parents had legal custody of me, I spent the majority of the first six years of my life in the care of my maternal grandparents. One could say that they were my parents because it was with them that I began to understand who Christ was and how He would impact my life. Everything that I recall before the age of six years old took place while I was in the care of my grandparents. I really do not remember anything that occurred before the age of four years old.

My grandfather was a deacon in the church where he later became a Minister. He was a praying man who prayed night and day. Late at night, when everyone had gone to bed, but me, I would hear him praying and calling on the name of Jesus. It seemed as if he prayed for hours. He was a man with a strong faith in God. When I was young, I had frequent nose bleeds. Immediately, my grandfather would grab his Bible, put me on his knee, hold my nose with a brown paper bag, and start reading scriptures from the Bible and praying over me. Instantly, my nose would stop bleeding. As I grew older, the nose bleeds stopped occurring. One of the main things that I do remember is that going to church was not an option. Every time the doors of the church were opened, my grandparents required that we attended the service. At five years old, I was very productive in Sunday school. I loved going. It gave me peace. Yes, PEACE, "And the peace of God, which passeth all understanding, shall keep your hearts and minds through Christ Jesus;"

Philippians 4:7. Peace from the verbal abuse and the physical abuse that I witnessed almost daily when I wasn't with my grandparents. This is where my actual spiritual journey began. I am grateful for the serenity and the security that my grandparents provided for me.

When I was with my parents, my life seemed as if it was in a downward swirl. I remember crying all the time. I was always stressed out and worried about my mother. My mother was a hard- working woman, but she was an alcoholic. Whenever she drank alcohol, she drank until she was drunk. Once she became drunk, she would start crying. The drunken crying would result in her falling all over the house. Of course, I did not understand why she was crying nor drinking to the state of drunkenness. Consequently, I would begin crying and worrying. I just wanted her to be okay. Five years old was just too young to be stressing and worrying as much as I did. Constantly, I tried to understand why my mother would drink and cry as much as she did. Now that I am older, and I have experienced some things, I do understand. That was her way of dealing with the hurt and the pain that she was enduring from her unhappy marriage to my father and the verbal, physical, emotional, and mental abuse she endured at his hands.

When I was younger, my father was in the Navy. I do not remember him being around much except for my birthday and various other occasions. He and my mother were married, but he lived in another state with another woman. I really did not understand that either. So many things that did not make sense at that time make a lot of sense now. He had many women in various states. He also had many children who lived in various states and whom I never met. At one point in time in our lives, my mother and I shared a home with one of her younger sisters and her child. It was pleasant until my aunt married a man who was in the Air Force, and he moved in. After he moved in, everything changed drastically. He started moving in all his family; his brother, and his daughter to be exact.

Whenever my mother, my aunt, and my aunt's husband were working, they left my aunt's husband's brother to watch us. That was mistake number one. He was a bad person. He would do "bad things" to us. We were young and did not know what was really going on, but I did know that what he was doing he should not be doing. I went to my mother and told her what had been going on. My mother became very upset and confronted my abuser. Well, you know the story; he accused me of lying, and so did his brother, who was not there when his brother was molesting us repeatedly and showing us his genitals and his bare butt. Because I told, my aunt's husband started mistreating me, being very abusive and mean to me. My mother told my father what happened to me. My father was so angry that he attempted to kill my molester. Yes, my father attempted to kill that man, but his brother, my aunt's husband, jumped in the way, and the bullet hit him in the leg. For the remainder of his life, my aunt's husband walked with a limp due to the damage caused by that bullet on that day.

From that point forward, I began to suffer with low self-esteem and a low self-confidence. I just did not feel the same as I did before all of this took place. All I know is that every time I was verbally abused by that man or mistreated, it upset me emotionally. I did not know how to deal with these emotions or feelings. My mother's drinking escalated. It was just too much. Her drinking was so bad that there were times when I would miss the school bus. During this time, my bus stop was located at the old Lelia Ellis Elementary School. This school is now the LAMP building and where a homeless shelter is located. One morning, my mother dropped me off late and just left me because she was still drunk from the night before. I stood at the bus stop for what seemed like forever until an administrator from inside the school came outside and took me inside to determine where I was supposed to be. All I could do was cry because I was afraid, and I could not tell them much. I was only five years old. This experience was traumatic to me. There were not any cell phones back then, and we did not have a house phone. Eventually, the administrators determined that I attended Sallas Mahone Elementary School and ensured that I arrived there safely.

By the time I reached the second grade, we moved on the south side of town. We were living in a two-bed room apartment in what was then called Forest Manor. I hated living there. I almost never went outside. If I did decide to sit on the back porch, I always had to fight. Don't ask me why because I did not know any of the people who lived out there, and I did not care to know them. Every time I came out the door, I had to defend myself against every mean and hateful child that lived in the apartment complex. Not only did I have to fight to defend myself, but I constantly intervened when my mother and father were fighting. I wouldn't exactly say a fight because my father was always physically and verbally abusing my mother. My stomach stayed tied up in knots from all the fighting. I cannot remember a day that went by that my father was not beating my mother or cursing her and calling her everything but a child of God. I was a nervous wreck and those darn bad children who were always trying to fight me did not make matters any better.

I always worried about my mother especially when I was at school because I was not around to protect her from my father. I was so afraid that one day they were going to call me to the office and tell me that my father had killed my mother. One morning while I was preparing to go to school, my mother was calling my name. Immediately, I ran to see what was wrong. She was laying on the floor naked, sweating and crying. She instructed me to run and go get one of the neighbors with whom she was friends, so I did as I was instructed. The neighbor came to see about my mother and sent me on to school. I could hear and see the ambulance as I was walking across the street to school. All I could think about was my mother. I cried all day long until I got called to the office. My heart started pounding, and my stomach started hurting. I was scared that my mother died because what no one knew was that my father had beat the HELL out of her the night before. My mother was in the hospital, and the doctor determined that she was pregnant. Consequently, she lost the baby. My mother never reported to the doctor that my father had beat her, and that was probably why she lost the baby.

All our neighbors knew my father was verbally and physically abusive to my mother. He did not care where he beat her. One night he beat her all the way down the street. People were looking out of their windows and standing in their doorways watching and shaking their heads, but no one tried to stop him or call the police. Sometimes, I would yell, "Please stop beating my mama!" He would then start yelling and cursing at me and threaten to beat the hell out of me. As a result, we were evicted from our apartment. We were homeless and had to go live with one of my mother's friends, a lady who attended church with us. We lived with my mother's friend for almost two years.

Finally, we moved into a two-bedroom apartment. I was nine years old and in the fourth grade. Before we were evicted, my mother had another child. Although I was only nine years old, I found myself taking on adult responsibilities such as cooking, cleaning, and baby-sitting my baby sister. My mother worked two jobs and was hardly ever home. I spent a lot of time alone and afraid because I was home alone. During this time, I began to cry out to God a lot. I literally cried and yelled as loudly as I could to God.

My father was always out with other women drinking and clubbing. My mother was always working. Although my mother worked hard, her income alone was not enough to pay the bills, keep food on the table, and ensure that I had decent clothes and shoes. Therefore, I usually went without until it was a dire necessity. I guess you could ask what my father was doing. He was not doing anything to provide for our household, but he did continue to physically abuse my mother and take her money for his and his other women's pleasure. My father had another child who was older than I was. It was obvious that she was his favorite child and that I was his least favorite which added kerosene to the fire that was already brewing inside of me mentally and emotionally. I remember wearing shoes and clothes until they couldn't be worn again, but my father would take my older sister shopping at quality clothing stores and buy her name brand clothes and shoes. They would bring these clothes and shoes back to the house and show them to me. He would leave me home alone feeling abandoned and rejected. Not once did they bring me a shirt or a pair of shoes. This made me even angrier, bitter, and resentful. As the anger, bitterness, and resentment increased, I began to cry out more to God. It was during this time in my life that I truly learned to depend on God and trust him to get me through this hell on earth that I was living in.

Church became my place of comfort because it was here that I found serenity. I gave my life to Christ at age nine. For the first time in years, I felt a sense of peace. It was now that Hebrews 11:1 became evident to me. According to Hebrews 11:1, "Now Faith is the substance of things hoped for, the evidence of things not seen". Hope became a valuable concept in my life. My hope gave me a feeling of expectation that things would get better. They just had to, and I felt within my spirit that my trust in God was the key to my life getting better.

Better did not happen immediately. In fact, things became worse. We had finally moved into a three-bedroom home. My mother had another child, and I became teenage mother to both of my younger sisters. My dad became even more abusive to my mother more than ever before. Now, he was also verbally and physically abusing me. I not only witnessed the many beatings that my mother endured, but I was also being beaten. In my eyes, my father was inhumane. I often inquired of my mother if she was sure that he was my biological father because of the way he mistreated me. He acted as if he hated me and that is the way he treated me. The anger, bitterness, and resentment was at an all-time high. I begin to sleep with a butcher's knife under my pillow at night. My father was beating my mother every chance he could, and she did not defend herself. He even began to bring his girlfriends to our home in utter disrespect to my mother. I lived and learned all of this. I longed to be loved and treated with kindness and warmth.

High school was a blur. It was also an escape from the verbal and physical abuse that I was dealing with daily. I did not have many friends because I was afraid to trust anyone. I did not want anyone to know or find out about my life behind closed doors. Because I was so angry and bitter, I became antisocial, but I participated in about every club at the high school. Ironically, I could hide the physical bruises, but not the mental and emotional scars that were left. If only they knew how I had been beaten the night before or how I had my head smashed continuously on our concrete floor just minutes before going to school. At age seventeen, I left home with the clothes on my back and the shoes on my feet. I was tired. I could not take another insult or another lick. I was now homeless. The night before my dad beat my mother very badly, and he also beat me. I can remember it as if it was yesterday. He came home in a rage about something that had happened in the streets. I assume with one of his many women. My mother always got punished for their misdeeds, and so did I.

This night, I witnessed my dad stomping my mother in her face and in her stomach with his hard-bottomed shoes. This traumatized me, and I began to scream and holler at him to please leave my mother alone. What did I do that for? He ran after me like a mad man. He called me every profane name he could think of. He told me that I was not anything and that I never would be. Then he proceeded to beat me down to the floor with his fists. Repeatedly, he beat my head on the concrete floor as if he was trying to kill me. Finally, he took his hard-bottomed shoe and stomped me in my stomach as hard as he could. I lost consciousness. By the time I came to, he was gone. I got up and climbed in my bed. I did not sleep at all that night. One thing that I did know was that I knew that this would be the last time that he put his hands on me.

The next morning, I got up early and dressed as if I was preparing to go to school. I got in my car, and I drove to a friend's house. I requested to use the phone to call my grandmother whom I loved dearly. I contacted my grandmother, and I told her what happened. My grandmother instructed me to come to her house. I did not attend school that day. I was too distraught. My head was hurting, my stomach was hurting, and my face was swollen. My grandparents and two of my aunts were living in a one-bedroom shack in Naylor, GA. The house was very small, but it was filled with lots of love. As I drove to Naylor, I cried vehemently. I did not have any idea what would happen now. All I knew was that I had to get out of there and never go back. When I pulled into the driveway, my grandmother was standing on the back porch waiting for me. Before I could get out of the car, she held her arms out for me to come to her, and I did. She held me, hugged me, and assured me that everything would be all right. My grandmother told me that I had made her the happiest woman in the world that day because I got out of that house of abuse. She stated, "You will never go back there. If your mama wants to stay there and let him kill her then let her, but you will not." I spent the remainder of that school year and the following year which was my senior year of high school living from one relative's home to another. My dad sent threats of harm to me every day through my frightened mother. He wouldn't allow me to get my clothes or my shoes.

I spent the remainder of my junior year and senior year in high school with a heaviness in my heart; thus, my faith and my hope in the Lord grew even stronger. Romans 5: 2-5 states "Through him we have also obtained access by faith into this grace in which we stand, and we rejoice in hope of the glory of God more than that, we rejoice in our sufferings, knowing that sufferings produce endurance, and endurance produces character, and character produces hope, and hope does not put us to shame, because God's love has been poured into our hearts through the Holy Spirit who has been given to us".

Thus, began my quest to find love and be loved. It appears I searched for love in many faces, but they were always the wrong faces. It took many years of bad relationships and broken hearts for me to realize that I had been looking for love in all the wrong places. I married whom I thought would be my King, and I in turn would be his Queen. The marriage was my worst nightmare. My husband spent 99.99% of our marriage in prison. I was miserable and very unhappy. Being married to him became intolerable. As a result, I became suicidal due to overwhelming feelings that I was stuck in this unhappy marriage due to my spiritual beliefs. The Lord saw me in my broken and contrite state of mind. It was then that Jeremiah 29:11 became so important to me and my way of life. Jeremiah 29:11 states "For I know the plans I have for you, declares the Lord, plans to prosper you and not to harm you, to give you a **HOPE** and a future". The Lord placed true men and women of God in my life and path to give me spiritual guidance and spiritual direction. Consequently, I divorced my husband whom I had been married to for eight years. I was relieved, and I felt free from that bondage.

Before my divorce was finalized, I became involved with a man from New Orleans. He was mean as the devil. It was two years into the relationship that his true nature began to flourish. I thought that I had been given another chance at true love, but it was just the opposite. This man was verbally and physically abusive. Sound familiar? I became my mother. All my life I always stated that I would never be like my mother, yet here I was, living in the exact same situation that God delivered my mother from. I really did not understand how or why I became caught up in such a situation as this. I was praying to God for a husband. God heard me, but so did the enemy.

Satan was on a quest to kill me by any means necessary. I dated this man for four years and towards the end of the relationship, the abuse became brutal. It was now that I was given a prophetic word from the Lord that this man whom I was involved with was an assignment from the enemy to kill and destroy me. He attempted on several occasions, but the last attempt opened my eyes. He literally kidnapped me and held me captive. He told me he was going kill me, and I knew he meant it. Ironically, he went to church with me and my kids earlier that day. He even took us out to dinner. After dinner, we all went to my house, sat around and talked, and laughed. Suddenly, he changed.

While in captivity, he choked me to the point of unconsciousness, he stabbed me in the neck with a ballpoint pen, he beat me with his fists all over my body, and he raped me. Throughout the beatings, I began to pray aloud, and the beating became worse, but I know God heard me. After he raped me, he became insanely calm and let me go. When I got away, I went home. I ran straight to the bathroom and began thanking God and crying out to him for sparing my life. I took a shower and got in my bed. I cried all night long. The next day, I went to work.

Yes, I attempted to file a report with the police, but they informed me that it was my word against his. I was also informed that I would have to secure an attorney to take out a restraining order on him. I did not have any money for all of that. I did not know what to do or who to turn to. That man terrorized me for several weeks. Every time he came to my house, I would call the law. Finally, a female police officer came to my hous, and she gave me explicit instructions on how to deal with the devil in flesh who was terrorizing me. I did exactly as she instructed me to do, and the visits to my home, the visits to my job, and the constant calls to my job and home stopped. God allowed me to go through what I went through to turn my attention back to Him. It became evident that God was the only one who could deliver me from the hands of the enemy. I had been sleeping with the enemy, and he was playing for keeps.

Physically, I had bruises all over my body. Emotionally, I was terrified and scarred. Three years after the incident, I was still traumatized. I stopped communicating with any men at all. I refused to date anyone. I just wanted to be left alone. Every year for three years to be exact, I would cry uncontrollable two weeks before the date of the anniversary of that final incident in which he had attempted to kill me. It was so bad until all I could do was lie in bed and cry. By the fourth year, I was tired of that impending feeling of doom which was associated with what he had done to me. I wanted to be free. I prayed and asked God to heal me from this trauma, and He did. It has been ten years now, and I can't even remember the date it happened although I will always remember *what* happened.

Consequently, I stopped looking for love. I had lost hope of finding my true love, but I gained the hope that he would find me. My prayers became focused on mental, physical, and emotional healing. According to Romans 8:24-25, "For in this hope we were saved. Now hope that is seen is not hope. For who hopes for what he sees? But if we hope for what we do not see, we wait for it with patience". That is exactly what I did. I prayed, I hoped, and I waited patiently. I did not look for love anymore because love found me.

It had been five years since I even attempted to date or become romantically involved with anyone. Frankly, I was lonely and wanted a husband, but I was afraid to love again. Unexpectedly, love pursued me, and I did what my instincts told me to do. I ran, but love followed me. Eventually, the Holy Spirit stopped me and reminded me of my prayers. I listened, and I stopped. I have been in a relationship for two and half years now. I have watched God bring about changes in him as well as in myself that only God can do. I thought I was ready for marriage, but life experiences and prayer helped me to realize that I was still a work in progress. I am thankful that God placed James Crawford in my life to impact my life and allow me another chance to love and be loved.

My entire life has been very challenging. Statistically, I should have been a street walker or even worse, a drug addict. I was exposed to a lot of inappropriate things as an impressionable child. If the cliché "children learn what they live and live what they learn" held true, statistics would be accurate. I did not know that I was chosen even then for such a task as this. I had been chosen, and God had plans for me. I continue to pray and submit to God. My faith and my hope increases daily due to prayer and submission to God. "Be careful for nothing, but in everything by prayer and supplication with thanksgiving let your requests be made known unto God. And the peace of God, which passeth all understanding, shall keep your hearts and minds through Jesus Christ," Proverbs 4:6-7.

I do not look like what I have been through. Many people probably would not believe the process it took for me to get to where I am currently. Even now my life is not where I feel it should be, but it is not where it once was. My faith in God has sustained me and kept me throughout my spiritual journey. Thus, everything I went through as a child set the premise for the vision, **VISION OF HOPE**, which God gave me to help young men and women who have lost their way and lost hope in finding their way to become productive and successful citizens in their community by restoring their hope in their own abilities. "Know that wisdom is such to your soul, if you find it, there will be a future, and your hope will not be cut off", Proverbs 24:14.

Childhood Traumas

Demetria Hill Cannady, PhD, LPC

There are numerous types of trauma which can occur in childhood: The Natural Child Traumatic Stress Network (www.nctsn.org/trauma-types) listed the following: community violence; complex trauma; domestic violence; early childhood trauma; medical trauma; natural disasters; neglect; physical abuse; refugee trauma; school violence; sexual abuse; terrorism; and traumatic grief. "**Community violence** consisting of predatory violence and violence between people that's not family. It can also involve shootings, rape, stabbings, and beatings. Children can be victims, witnesses, or perpetrators. I recall a friend of mine sharing that she never went outside because every time she did, she had to fight the children in the apartment complex. This would be a prime example of community violence. Another example would be that of gang members; if you're not representing the "right" gang or not a gang member at all, this could present as a problem, especially if you're trying to gain access to a certain area which is deemed "gang territory." **Complex trauma** is the exposure to multiple or prolonged traumatic events and the impact of exposure on their development. There are several forms of complex trauma, to name a few: psychological maltreatment, neglect, physical abuse, sexual abuse, and domestic violence. There are also chronic forms of complex trauma and this begins in early childhood and by the people who are your primary caretakers," (www.nctsn.org). Many of these individuals encounter Department of Family and Children Services because there has been a report made and an investigation completed which adds additional trauma of the child being removed from the natural home and placed with strangers even though the "strange" new environment is safer than the home environment. All the child know is that they have been taken away from their parents whether the reasons were beneficial for safety or not.

"**Domestic Violence** is the intimate partner violence, domestic violence, or battering of an individual which includes the actual or threatened physical or sexual violence or emotional abuse between adults in intimate relationships. Domestic violence can include physical harm in a heterosexual or homosexual relationship and can be with a former or current significant other/spouse. There are three to ten million children that are exposed to domestic violence in the United States every year and most of these children are under the age of eight years old," (www.nctsn.org/trauma-types). I remember when my mother was married to her second husband, and this relationship being a domestic violence relationship, with my mother as the victim. I can't begin to imagine the trauma she received as the result of being the recipient of the abuse and by her daughter witnessing the abuse (hearing), but I remember being an indirect victim at nine years old and seeing more than she thought that I did. There would be times where I would be in my room, and I would hear the arguments because she refused to give him money (he was an addict). The arguments would turn into fights because she wouldn't give him money to feed his addiction.

I felt helpless and enraged as I would think of ways to protect my mother and bring harm to him, thus ending her pain, my indirect pain, and his life. I used to think about which knife in the kitchen drawer that I would use to kill him while he slept during his drug-induced comas. He ended up getting incarcerated, so I didn't have to bring my plans to fruition (Thank God!). I grew up to be an angry and aggressive teenager, young adult, and adult. I vowed that no man was going to put his hands on me, and if he did, I would kill him. I was slapped one time by my daughter's biological father, and I tried my best to harm him by having target practice, throwing knives, at him. He was great at ducking, dodging, and getting out the house before a knife connected with him.

I was able to release all the years of anger when I entered a relationship with my now husband. I would attempt to argue with him when we first began dating, and he would walk out the house, get in his car, and leave. Each time I tried to argue, he would leave. It's hard to argue by yourself. To date and sixteen years later, we don't argue. I say what I must say, he may respond, and that's the end of it. There may be a day or two of silence if I'm really upset, but he taught me how not to argue, and for that I'm grateful. He healed the once angry woman that I was, and our children have never experienced us argue or fight.

"**Early childhood trauma** is trauma which occurs between 0-6 years of age. This trauma can be physical abuse, sexual abuse, natural disasters, accidents, war, painful medical procedures, or the sudden loos of a parent or caregiver. **Medical trauma** is the mind or body reaction to pain, injury, significant injury, "invasive" medical procedures (surgery), or treatments (burn care) that children view as frightening. **Natural disasters** can invoke trauma especially if it causes a child and their family to be displaced and/ or they lose love ones during the natural disasters," (www.nctsn.org/trauma-types).

"**Neglect** is when the parent or caregiver does not provide the child with the care he/she needs, to include: food, clothing, shelter, medical treatment, mental health treatment, medications which the doctor has prescribed, inadequate education (consistency with school attendance and or special accommodation at school); poor and/or inadequate supervision; exposure to dangerous environments; and putting a minor child out the home with nowhere else to go. **Physical abuse** is the causing or attempting to cause physical pain or injury by punching, beating, kicking, burning, or harming a child in other ways; inappropriate punishment; and inappropriate acts which can or may lead to death. **Sexual abuse** is a wide range of sexual behaviors that takes place between a child and an older person or between a child and another child/adolescent; bodily contact such as sexual kissing, touching, fondling genitals, and intercourse. Sexual abuse does not always involve contact, it can be someone exposing their nude body to you, pressuring an individual to have sex, and exploitation of an individual for the purposes of prostitution or pornography," (www.nctsn.org).

"**School violence** includes fatal and nonfatal student or teacher victimization, threats to or injury of students, fights at school, and students carrying weapons to school; school violence is any behavior that violates a school's educational mission or climate of respect or jeopardizes the intent of the school to be free of aggression against persons or property, drugs, weapons, disruptions, and disorder. **Traumatic grief** occurs following the sudden, unexpected, or anticipated death of someone important to the child when the child perceives the experience as traumatic. There were a few other childhood traumas mentioned which very rarely affects the population we serve: refugee trauma and terrorism," (www.nctsn.org/trauma-types).

The National Pain Survey Report reported percentages of trauma which children experience:

- Emotional Abuse- 44%

- Bullying- 35%

- Sexual Abuse- 28%

- Witness to Violence- 24%

- Physical Abuse- 23%

- Death of a Parent- 17%

(www.americannewsreport.com)

If you are interested to know whether you experienced trauma while growing up, you can take the ACEs. The study (ACEs) focuses on ten areas of trauma (www.acestudy.com). These ten areas are psychological abuse; physical abuse; sexual abuse; emotional neglect; physical neglect; loss of parent; mother treated violently; substance abuse; mental illness; and criminal behavior in the household. You may surprise yourself with the answers.

Most of that which affected us in childhood continues to affect us as adults, especially if there was no therapy involved and if we didn't share our truth with at least one great friend or family member that would keep our secrets. Childhood haunts us into adulthood. A traumatized child usually grows into an angry, promiscuous, and/or drug addict adult because of the lack of coping skills to deal with the pain of the past. While completing this book, I watched the movie, "*For Colored Girls*," and as an African woman and therapist, this movie triggered many emotions because I could indirectly identify what most of the women in the movie was experiencing or had experienced. Most of these women have been my friends and former clients, and while they may not have had the exact same experience, the experiences were similar as black women with unaddressed therapeutic issues.

References:

Adverse Childhood Experiences (ACE), 1998. Retrieved from: https://www.acestudy.com

National Pain Report Survey, 2014. Childhood Trauma and Adult Pain: Is There a Connection? Retrieved from https://www.americannewsrpeort.com

The Natural Child Traumatic Stress Network, 2017. Community Violence. Retrieved from: https://www.nctsn.org/trauma-types.

The Natural Child Traumatic Stress Network, 2017. Complex Trauma. Retrieved from: https://www.nctsn.org/trauma-types.

The Natural Child Traumatic Stress Network, 2017. Domestic Violence. Retrieved from: https://www.nctsn.org/trauma-types.

The Natural Child Traumatic Stress Network, 2017. Early Childhood Trauma. Retrieved from: https://www.nctsn.org/trauma-types.

The Natural Child Traumatic Stress Network, 2017. Medical Trauma. Retrieved from: https://www.nctsn.org/trauma-types.

The Natural Child Traumatic Stress Network, 2017. Natural Disasters. Retrieved from: https://www.nctsn.org/trauma-types.

The Natural Child Traumatic Stress Network, 2017. Neglect. Retrieved from: https://www.nctsn.org/trauma-types.

The Natural Child Traumatic Stress Network, 2017. Physical Abuse. Retrieved from: https://www.nctsn.org/trauma-types.

The Natural Child Traumatic Stress Network, 2017. School Violence. Retrieved from: https://www.nctsn.org/trauma-types.

The Natural Child Traumatic Stress Network, 2017. Sexual Abuse. Retrieved from: https://www.nctsn.org/trauma-types.

The Natural Child Traumatic Stress Network, 2017. Terrorism. Retrieved from: https://www.nctsn.org/trauma-types.

The Natural Child Traumatic Stress Network, 2017. Traumatic Grief. Retrieved from: https://www.nctsn.org/trauma-types.

Eyvonne Pooler was born and raised in Dublin, Laurens County Georgia and attended the Dublin City Schools. She furthered her education at Mercer University obtaining a Bachelor of Science in Human Services, and Troy University with a Master's in Education Counseling and Psychology. She completed her PhD in Counseling from Capella University. She is a Licensed Professional Counselor and Master Addiction Counselor in the State of Georgia. In addition, she is CEO/President of E & A Cares Counseling Consultant Services, LLC. She is an active member of Alpha Kappa Alpha Sorority Incorporated through Phi Delta Omega Chapter of Vidalia, Georgia.

Dr. Pooler is an Associate Professor at Liberty University Online. She loves teaching as it affords her the opportunity to encourage students in their academic endeavors. She also loves serving! She has served on various boards as committee member, president, as well as chair and continues to serve.

Lastly, she believes the Word of God is a living document that serves as a guide for her life and teaches her that "Service to Others" is highly recommended from God. Two of her favorite verses read -

"For God is not unjust so as to overlook your work and the love that you have shown for His name in SERVING the saints, as you still do," Hebrews 6:10.

"He that dwells in the secret place of the Most-High shall ABIDE under the shadow of the Almighty," Psalm 91:1.

Dr. Pooler as she is known, and her husband, Andrew, have two sons and one daughter. They also have two beautiful granddaughters, ages eight and ten. Her favorite pastime is spending quality time with family, reading, volunteering, and traveling. She is also active members in her church where she enjoys worshiping and serving God.

Warm Regard,
Dr. Pooler

Mental Illness and Depression Resides in both Secular World and the Church

Dr. Eyvonne Pooler, LPC, MAC

As I sit contemplating where I should begin in sharing the relatively impactful depressive disorders, how it can impede one's life, and the affect it has on both secular and the church culture, I can't avoid explaining the several types of depression. There are diverse types that I would like to focus on very briefly. Stay with me as I attempt to lead you on this pathway of insightfulness as it relates to mental illness in both secular and church culture. It is my hope that you will find many nuggets helpful for yourself, a close family or friend, and/or even your frienemy.

There were times in my life that I felt sadness. I recall in retrospect, attempting to get in touch with my emotions because of the potential impact it can have on my life. I had to stop and think about what I was feeling. My thoughts were to stay in control, dominate my emotions, and speak to the issue. Practice deep breathing and cognitive reframing. I breathed and followed every fiber of oxygen permeating my entire being. It was not easy challenging those emotions. Thus, those mixed moods had strong intentions to invade my life.

At that time, it was quite difficult for me to effectively analyze and identify the root cause of my mood(s). I was determined to channel my thoughts toward positive thinking, cognitive reframing. However, to no avail! I knew it was vital to understand where the feelings existed internally or where the triggers existed externally. Could it be external or internal causes of my seemingly untamed emotions and sadness? No, I thought. I am a church member. I'm not to show my depressed emotions nor discuss it as this resonates as a lack of faith for my healing. I chose to challenge that concept and move in action for the betterment of myself.

It fact, my thoughts immediately attempted to think critically about how to challenge my emotions. Why feel that you are in this alone? You are not the only individual experiencing sadness. Every individual who breathes, lives on this side of the planet, has, too, experienced sadness. This feeling was very common, I convinced myself, and not a rare occurrence. Thus, I realized again in my analysis, this does not constitute clinical depression. There were many experiences which occurred in my life while sitting next to my fellow church member, I pretended to be okay. I was sitting in the church pews weekly, attending every service when the doors opened. I resolved that my sadness was a matter of my perceptions and me not putting in the work to rectify the issue.

It was essential for me to understand the differences between clinical depression and sadness to effectively recognize what was occurring in my life. Whether my mood was a factor of clinical depression or sadness, the key factor was for me to understand how to bring appropriate resources or connect with another entity who held them. Sadness is a normal emotion and can make life more interesting as it is a part of life. How, you may ask? It affords you the opportunity to turn within and find new discoveries. However, if not mindful, sadness may lead one to depression if a shift occurs in the opposite direction! Whether I was just sad or clinically depressed, it was vital for me to act and seek the appropriate resources to improve my mood for the betterment of my mental health.

The term, mental illness, can be a scary thought to categorize one's self, loved ones, or a close friend as it encompasses a broad selection of unforeseen internal challenges. If you look around in the workforce, church, community, even family, most likely there is someone who silently suffers from depression and/or mental illness. To name a few types of disorders associated with depression, which is the disorder the adversary uses to impede your mental progress, is conducive for the understanding of what type of depression one may experience.

Major Depression Disorder (MDD) is most common. Depressive disorders present in various categories, and while there is a plethora in similarities to each type of depression, each has its own exclusive set of symptoms. MDD is a condition whose primary symptom is an overwhelming depressed mood for one month or more. Individuals with depressed mood are affected in all facets of their lives, including work, home life, relationship, friendship, and church. This kind of depression makes it difficult to participate in activities or self-interest you once enjoyed. It can be challenging to put forth efforts and get motivated about life.

There are other types of depressive disorder such as dysthymia, adjustment disorder with depressed mood, seasonal affective, bipolar, postpartum to name a few. Depression is a serious matter, yes! And, it can be found in the church on the pews of many church goers. Therefore, not only do I want to discuss information regarding depression, but how it is prevalent in the church.

Dysthymia is very like MDD (Major Depressive Disorder); however, symptoms occur for much longer periods, two years or more. This type is considered a chronic form of depression. Treating an individual with this type of depression can be challenging. Usually, many treatment modalities have been used, but to no avail.

Adjustment disorder with Depressed Mood is another type of depressive disorder. The condition associated with this disorder is that individuals are not able to adjust to a very stressful event. Here, the individual needs support in their lives during the stressful time; treatment is time limited and simple.

Seasonal Affective Disorder is when individuals suffer symptoms of a Major Depressive Disorder only during a specific time of year, usually winter. Seasonal depression is called seasonal affective disorder (SAD). While there are many types of depression, some types of this condition seem to be related to change in the length of days or seasonality.

Bipolar Disorder, is considered a symptom of depression, but not a form of depression. Bipolar disorder is considered a mood disorder. This disorder is characterized by swings of a person's mood from depression to mania (loss of energy, feelings of, sometimes, on top of the world). There are so many other forms of depression, but let's move into the true meat of depression and its impact on Christians' functionality both physically and spiritually. Mental illness is prevalent in both the secular and church culture, yet secretively held within. Raised awareness is important to removing the stigma associated with the term "mental illness." Whether through personal or acquaintance, those of us whose lives have been affected by mental health struggles understand that receiving help from a trained professional is vital to one's physical health, yet, seeking help is the hardest part. Please, get help! Getting help will afford you the opportunity to thrive in your best self. There are many biblical heroes who experienced depression as well as their offspring. Which do you believe King David experienced? Major Depressive Disorder (MDD), Dysthymic, and/or Bipolar? David raised awareness of his feelings and others must do so as well to begin the healing process.

As far back as 200 B.C., the church, or synagogue has been a hospital where God met the needs of His people and to start the mending process. Now, I understand that God moved in various places in the biblical times; however, God always placed emphasis on the church. There was much beckoning by Jesus, himself, to bring the sick, the lame, to the church to be healed, an invitation that is so often rejected by those who believe they are just fine. I also believe that many individuals in both the secular and church culture would rather wait on God to heal their wounds. I am speaking of those pains developed in your childhood, adolescence, or early adult life. If you do not put into action your efforts to minimize those hurts and pains, it most likely will linger in your mind and challenge your self-esteem and confidence in your God-given ability. It is written that God is a gentle Spirit; therefore, He will not intrude your will (heart) to push you into getting help for past hurts. You must step forward, and He will meet you there as He has for countless others who suffer with feelings of sadness, loneliness, distorted negative thinking. He did it for those listed in the Bible throughout to current heroes.

I've often heard individuals equate, in their minds, depression to a room engulfed in flames, and you can't breathe because the smoke smothers the very core of your mindset. Everything seems unbearable. The mindset begins to uphold negative distorted thinking. Seemingly, negative thoughts dominate your whole self and control every aspect of you on a social and/or private level. I've talked to many individuals struggling with depression and many have said it feels like you're in a box or hit a brick wall, and there is absolutely no outlet. Thus, it is solid brick wall that has risen to a place greater that you can ever grasp. Depression is more than a prolonged case of blues; it interferes with one's normal daily activities, alter healthy thinking, and influence you to believe that you are alone. Allow me to share words I often quote as I listen to individuals explain their struggles and challenges with depression. It's my hope that these words will incite a motivation within you so strong that you're confident any challenge can be conquered. I want you to think about how you think. Think about your current perception of your mental health.

Think about your past and present life as you read:

You settle for and believe every thought now where you use to not;

break the cycle of thoughts; try to find some source of light,

try to name one thing you like;

it's so easy to give up on what you once liked;

your confidence once soared high;

but now it's so easy to second-guess everything you do with a sigh;

sad feelings knew how to pass; there's a light that await to make you glad;

but, now it seems like it's every day you're sad; everyday, it seems like you're sad.

Depression is a serious disorder that can impact the lives of anyone. It does not have respect of one's name, culture, accomplishments, or religious affiliation. One thing I have learned in my profession is that depression can significantly interrupt the lives of anyone. If individuals do not have the appropriate tools and know how to deal and/or cope with life stressors, negative thoughts, and/or low self-esteem, the risk of depression may occur. Sometimes, depression is solely connected with heritage. This means that there is a family line that struggles with mental illness and/or clinical depression. One way to understand depression from a hereditary standpoint is to review the term chemically imbalanced. Chemical imbalance is said to cause emotional distress and disturbances. Although clinical studies and medical observations have been able to identify several chemical inconsistencies, it appears that many confuse the two differences, chemical imbalances vs. chemical inconsistencies, which both tends to occur in individuals who experience symptoms related to mental illness. Mental health is a serious matter.

Did you know that King David, a man after God's own heart, was depressed? He opens the verses of Psalm 13 with "How long, Oh Lord will you forget me forever? How long do I have to wrestle with my thoughts?" David felt that the challenge was too great to deal with alone. He expressed that dealing with his depression caused loneliness in his heart every day. Not only did

David experience depression but his offspring as well. His son, Solomon, expressed that he hated his life because the work that is done under the sun was grievous to him (Ecclesiastes 2:17). Should we respond surprise? We shouldn't reject the reality that mentally ill and depressed individuals occupy not only secular hospitals and clinics but reside within churches as well.

Studies reported that at least 25% of the U.S. population has struggled or currently struggles with depression for a considerable time and lack effective tools to help cope. It's important to state that chemical imbalances and other issues lead to mental illnesses. In my opinion, both the secular world and the church have neglected to engage the discussion surrounding mental illness and/or depression. Twenty-five percent is too high when discussing one's mental health and well-being.

Depression remains both accustomed and mysterious in the secular and church culture; not to mention those who share the pew with depressed persons. It is unfitting to say that only a few individuals have experienced depression. The feelings of, "I'm down," for no known reason, "I woke up on the wrong side of bed," syndrome should not be haphazardly stated. One thing we seldom think about is that there are individuals who sit on the pews of the church weekly, ministers too, struggling with mental illness or depression. Likewise, in the homes of individuals, husband, wife, even children who are struggling with depressed moods and do not understand how to rise out of the slope of depression. Both secular and church folks should confirm the value of medical and mental health treatment. In essence, mental illness and heath does not acknowledge family's beliefs. It can impact anyone. It is important to discuss depression.

Spiritual Depression is Real: As stated earlier, depression exist during B.C. King David stated, 'Be merciful unto me, O Lord, for I am in distress; my eyes grow weak with *sorrow*, my soul and body with grief." He further says, "My life is consumed by anguish and my years by groaning my strength fails because of my affliction, and my bones grow weak" (Psalms 31: 9 – 10). This segment clearly shows that David experienced some form of depressed mood. Spiritual Depression. What do you think David was feeling in the very depth of his spirit? His writings clearly provide us with a pass to discuss feelings of sadness, moods, and irritability, by addressing further his lamentation, "I am forgotten by them as though I were dead" (v.12). Severe depression is often beyond description; therefore, when such deep and painful feelings con not be explained, they cut to the heart of one's spiritual being.

We do not have to settle in the pain of depression. Like David, we must acknowledge our feelings and its impact on our emotions. Depression is not something that is "caught" or even "catches," thus, it starts with a perception (a thought). However, depression does have biological markers, for example, depletion of the neurotransmitters serotonin. I would be remiss to exclude "complexity of problem(s) that is related to past trauma, cultural situation, spiritual and religious concerns, losses, guilt and shame, medical problems, and so much more. These factors tend to lead to and incite feelings of depression. Unfortunately, depression is an illness and can be challenging as well as cause spiritual withdrawal. Depression can be caused by the individual, partially, actions. Think about the experiences of individuals who are deeply scarred by physical, emotional, or even sexual abuse.

Whether you are in the secular or church culture, getting treatment for mental illness is vital. There are treatment modalities that are effective in minimizing mental illness. Utilizing tools such as cognitive behavioral therapy and reality therapy, antidepressant medications, and prayer are excellent tools to become whole. It's almost a mystery that God has given you the resources by which to make progressive existences more pleasant. Please understand that God can heal mental illness with little efforts; however, He's given trained professionals the insight and instinct to see beyond the surface and provide effective tools to help both secular and the church cultures, especially for those who are in pain and struggling to get through life effectively and healthy without losing their identity.

As stated earlier, mental illness is stigmatized in both secular and the church culture. Perhaps, there are irrational ideas about it. Society tends to marginalize individuals with mental illness and/or depression which may be the cause why treatment is not sought. I'm led to believe due to concepts that if someone has mental illness or receives treatment he or she is unable to live a fruitful life. This is a myth and holds no truth for neither secular nor church culture; the concept that if one receives mental health for mental illness and/or depression; the stigma of spiritual weakness is a lack of faith. These are all myths.

I recall attending a church where the pastor identified a woman's mental illness as the spiritual forces like demon possessed and ignored or ruled out the cognitive or biological factors involves. Study shows that 25 percent of adults in the U.S. suffer from a diagnosable mental illness and statistics are not any different within the church. This is not a rare and marginal experience as mental illness and/or depression affects many. Therefore, individuals who suffer from mental illness and/or depression need to know they are not alone. There is hope and help acceptable even within the church.

It is applaudable for individuals to seek help for their mental illness and/or depression. Some may debate that the church should be able to reject depression and uphold the belief that their faith will aid in delivery of depression. This is very possible. However, it's okay to seek professional help for your mental wellbeing. However, it is reasonable to raise the question, how can one effectively serve God holistically if mental illness and depressive disorders are present? There will be challenges! If we confess, we all know someone close to us who is suffering with mental illness within the secular and the church culture. God is a healer. I am a strong believer of His ability to heal any condition. However, He wants us to display action. Every time, to uphold efficacy for our physical health, we must ensure to tend to our mental health.

Closing
Demetria Hill Cannady, PhD, LPC

In closing, this is the second of three books; two books with the women's perspective regarding their spirituality and mental health, and the third book will address the men's perspective of their mental health and spirituality. Even though it is my opinion that I am completing a divine assignment, I am also clear that this project has allowed me to process my own spirituality, mental health, and to process experiences which I had not spoken of within my own childhood. I feel my spiritual journey has been elevated to another level, and I am aware that there is more work that I am assigned to do in addition to writing these books on spirituality and mental health. This vision is still coming to fruition.

Book Two is an additional "conversation piece" regarding African American women, spirituality, and mental health, especially with all the events occurring in the world to date. Let's remove the stigma from mental health, mental illness, African Americans, and women, and allow ourselves to get the treatment that we need to be healthy and whole. Most of us desire to live an authentic life even if the authenticity happens later in our lives than we chose. What does it mean to be "whole" as a person? How can we ensure that we are living our best life while being true to ourselves? One thing that we can do is ensure that our bodies, mind, and thought processes are intact and that we are "whole." To become a "whole" person if you're not already, you must ensure that your emotional (mental health), spiritual health, physical health, intellectual health, and social circle are healthy.

When a piece of our "whole" person is out of sync, address it, and get the help needed so that you can have an optimal quality of life and/or return to your optimal quality of life. Address your physical health needs with your primary physician, nutritional health with a nutritionist or wellness specialist, spiritual health with your higher power and/or spiritual leader, and your emotional health needs with a therapist and/or psychiatrist, depending on the severity level of care needed. All the functional pieces make an individual "whole." I can suggest the following resources as it pertains to mental health needs and resources, as this is my area of expertise. If you know that you are not functioning at your optimal level, and you feel out of sync emotionally, here are a few mental health resources that you can utilize:

Hotline Numbers

- **Adolescent Suicide Hotline** 800-621-4000
- **Adolescent Crisis Intervention & Counseling Nine line** 1-800-999-9999
- **AIDS National Hotline** 1-800-342-2437
- **CHADD-Children & Adults with Attention Deficit/Hyperactivity Disorder** 1-800-233-4050
- **Child Abuse Hotline** 800-4-A-CHILD
- **Cocaine Help Line** 1-800-COCAINE (1-800-262-2463)
- **Domestic Violence Hotline** 800-799-7233
- **Domestic Violence Hotline/Child Abuse** 1-800-4-A-CHILD (800 422 4453)
- **Drug & Alcohol Treatment Hotline** 800-662-HELP
- **Ecstasy Addiction** 1-800-468-6933
- **Eating Disorders Center** 1-888-236-1188
- **Family Violence Prevention Center** 1-800-313-1310
- **Gay & Lesbian National Hotline** 1-888-THE-GLNH (1-888-843-4564)

- **Missing & Exploited Children Hotline** 1-800-843-5678
- **National Alliance on Mental Illness (NAMI)** 1-800-950-NAMI (6264)
- **Panic Disorder Information Hotline** 800- 64-PANIC
- **Post Abortion Trauma** 1-800-593-2273
- **Project Inform HIV/AIDS Treatment Hotline** 800-822-7422
- **Rape (People Against Rape)** 1-800-877-7252
- **Rape, Abuse, Incest, National Network (RAINN)** 1-800-656-HOPE (1-800-656-4673)
- **Runaway Hotline** 800-621-4000
- **Self-Injury (Information only)** (NOT a crisis line. Info and referrals only) 1-800-DONT CUT (1-800-366-8288)
- **Sexual Assault Hotline** 1-800-656-4673
- **Sexual Abuse - Stop It Now!** 1-888-PREVENT
- **STD Hotline** 1-800-227-8922

• **Gay & Lesbian Trevor Help Line Suicide** Prevention 1-800-850-8078	• **Suicide Prevention Lifeline** 1-800-273-TALK
• **Healing Woman Foundation (Abuse)** 1-800-477-4111	• **Suicide & Crisis Hotline** 1-800-999-9999
• **Help Finding a Therapist** 1-800-THERAPIST (1-800-843-7274)	• **Suicide Prevention - The Trevor Help Line** (Specializing in gay and lesbian youth suicide prevention). 1-800-850-8078
• **Incest Awareness Foundation** 1-888 -547-3222	• IMAlive-online crisis chat
• **Learning Disabilities - (National Center For)** 1-888-575-7373	• **Teen Helpline** 1-800-400-0900
	• **Victim Center** 1-800-FYI-CALL (1-800-394-2255)
	• **Youth Crisis Hotline** 800-HIT-HOME

National Alliance on Mental Illness (NAMI)
1-800-950-NAMI (6264)
www.nami.org

Mental Health America (MHA)
1-800-969-6642
www.mentalhealth.net

National Institute on Alcohol Abuse and Alcoholism NIAAA
www.niaaa.nih.gov

National Institute of Child Health and Human Development NICHD
www.nichd.nih.gov

National Institute on Drug Abuse NIDA
301-443-1124
www.nida.nih.gov

National Institute of Mental Health NIMH
1-866-615-6464
www.nimh.nih.gov

National Center for Complementary and Alternative Medicine
1-888-644-6226
http://nccam.nih.gov

Demetria Hill Cannady is the CEO of "A Work In Progress, LLC" a private practice in Valdosta, Georgia which focuses on Mental Health Wellness and Empowerment. She is a Licensed Professional Counselor and a Master Addictions Counselor in Georgia who counsels men, women, and children in the areas of mental health, substance abuse, behavior modification, trauma, and premarital/marriage counseling. Demetria is an Empowerment Coach who focuses on a variety of women's issues such as: self-esteem/ self-worth; relationships; single parent/blended families and family issues. Most issues can be resolved through coaching and/or counseling but requires communication; problem-solving; and goal setting.

Demetria Hill Cannady is a Certified Life Coach from the Life Coach Institute in Pensacola, Florida. She received her Bachelor Degree in Social Work and her Master's Degree in Mental Health Counseling from Fort Valley State University in Fort Valley, Georgia. Demetria holds a PhD in Human Services with a Specialization in Counseling Studies from Capella University in Minneapolis, Minnesota. She also holds Post-Certification in Contemporary Theory in Addictive Behavior and College Teaching; both obtained through Capella University in Minneapolis, Minnesota. Demetria is a Master Addictions Counselor and is facilitator for the "Prepare Enrich" which is a Premarital/ Marriage Curriculum which focuses on enhancing new marriages and/ or repairing broken marriages. Demetria Hill Cannady is married to Garry Cannady with a blended family of three adult daughters (one of whom is a newly enlisted member of the Air Force) and two biological sons together. In her spare time, she enjoys helping others to set goals, create vision boards, crochet, and playing Candy Crush.

www.ingramcontent.com/pod-product-compliance
Lightning Source LLC
Chambersburg PA
CBHW081156270326
41930CB00014B/3180